SHOPPING FOR FURNITURE ON THE INTERNET

Shopping for Furniture on the Internet

◆WHAT◆YOU◆MUST◆KNOW◆
◆BEFORE◆YOU◆BUY◆

By Leonard Bruce Lewin

LINDEN PUBLISHING CO. INC.
FRESNO, CA

SHOPPING FOR FURNITURE ON THE INTERNET:
WHAT YOU MUST KNOW BEFORE YOU BUY

by

Leonard Bruce Lewin

All rights reserved. No part of this book may be reproduced or transmitted in any form or by any means, electronic or mechanical, including photocopying, recording, or by any information storage and retrieval system, without written permission from the publisher, except for the inclusion of brief quotations in reviews.

© 2000 by Leonard Bruce Lewin

123456789
ISBN 0-941936-58-9

PRINTED IN THE UNITED STATES OF AMERICA

Lewin, Leonard Bruce, 1937-
　　Shopping for Furniture on the Internet : what you must know before you buy / by Leonard Bruce Lewin.
　　　　p. cm.
　　ISBN 0-941936-58-9
　　1. Furniture--Purchasing. 2. Shopping--Computer network resources. 3. Internet. I. Title.

TS885 .L46 2000
645.4'029'6--dc21

00-056909

LINDEN PUBLISHING

The Woodworker's Library

336 W. Bedford, Suite 107, Fresno CA 93711 USA
800-345-4447　www.lindenpub.com

Contents

Acknowledgments		7
Introduction		8
Chapter 1	"Good" and "Bad" Furniture	10
Chapter 2	Before You Start Shopping	12
Chapter 3	Shopping for Upholstered Furniture	24
Chapter 4	Shopping for Wood Furniture	44
Chapter 5	Understanding the Retailer	52
Chapter 6	Specialty Furniture	78
Chapter 7	Paying for Furniture	84

This book is dedicated to Elaine Weir Lewin: my wife, my best friend, my soulmate, and the love of my life. Thank you again, Peanut! I promise the next book will be about TFF.

DISCLAIMER: The information in this book is distributed "as is," without warranty. We have taken every prudent precaution in the preparation of this book and therefore neither the author nor Linden Publishing Co. Inc., shall have any liability to any person or entity with respect to any loss or damage caused or alleged to have been caused directly or indirectly by the information contained in this book.

IMPORTANT NOTICE: One of the most exciting aspects of the Internet is the fact that it is changing constantly. Every day new web sites are being added. New businesses are clamoring for your attention and, like any busy marketplace, the problem for these new businesses is how to get your attention. Your problem is how to stay current. Well, have I got a deal for you, and it won't cost a thing! Here at my web site, www.furnitureideas.com, I will be continually updating the new entries in the home furnishings field. To get this information, all you have to do is click on and see "What's New In Furniture." I hope you will take advantage of this opportunity to stay current. Of course you can also e-mail me at lewin@foothill.net. I say it often and I believe it totally: Information is power and the more information you have at your fingertips, the better a shopper you will be. It's my mission to help you stay informed, even after you are done reading this book.

Acknowledgments

As always, so many people contribute to any writer's efforts that to single out a few is to risk missing and offending the rest. My thanks go out to all, and especially to my publisher, Richard Sorsky. His encouragement and support have given me a showcase to present my views of a lifetime spent in a labor of love.

Foreword

During the 38 years I've been actively involved in the furniture industry, first as a manufacturer's representative for the Heritage/Morganton Furniture Company and then with the Drexel-Heritage Furniture Company, I have seen and done it all. I've traveled over 1,000,000 miles selling furniture to dealers big and small. I've unloaded the trucks and trained the salespeople. I've shopped the big stores in New York and the little shops in Idaho. I know the furniture outlets in North Carolina and went to school with the owners. I've been on the complaint calls in Oklahoma and the service calls in Texas. I've talked to consumer groups in Oregon, California, Colorado, and Arizona. I've worked the warehouse sales and changed the light bulbs. I sold the kids down the street their first sofa and the couple cross town their last bedroom set. I've managed stores, cleaned stores, built stores, and closed stores. I've done the advertising and the inventory. I've hired people and I've fired people. I've motivated, castigated, and stimulated salespeople, and slept by the side of the road more than once. I've seen the business change from a "personality" dominated tapestry of manufacturers and retailers to a corporate blanket of committees and computers. I've seen everything change and nothing change. But two constants remain: the consumer and the home. My 38 years of experience with both have convinced me, more than ever, that today's consumers are eager to take charge of their homes. Not in a passive "tell me what to do way," but as informed, involved, and active partners in making their homes exciting and fulfilling places. The Internet is going to be the gateway for all of us to achieve that level of involvement, and I am excited to hold open the door to it for my readers.

Leonard B. Lewin
April 2000
Fair Oaks, California

> Did you know that according to the National Retail Federation, Internet sales in 1998 totaled $8 billion? In 1999, sales totaled $20 billion, and in 2004, total sales are expected to reach $184 billion. Now that's a revolution!

Introduction:

The Internet— Another World!

Shopping for furniture on the Internet is going to become a better idea with each passing day. Right now, though, it is a bit like trying to shop for an automobile and not being able to buy Ford, General Motors, Chrysler, Honda, Toyota, Nissan, or Mercedes. If you can't buy any of the Big Guys, what's left? That is exactly what we are going to talk about.

At the moment we are at the beginning of a new revolution in retailing, and like any beginning, there are a great number of improvements needed. I have personally been disappointed in what I was finding in the way of furniture that can be bought on the Internet, but as I delved deeper into Internet shopping I realized I was being too critical of these early efforts. I was, in effect, missing the larger picture of what Internet shopping will become. What is coming in the world of Internet shopping is going to be so much better for consumers that I am eager to share it with you. But there is good news and bad news: The good news is that the Internet is going to open the world of furniture to you in all of its complexity, diversity, magic, and mystery. The bad news is that, even though you will have more information available to make choices, your need to be an informed shopper will be greater than ever before. Why? Simple. The amount of information that you will have to consider will be overwhelming. If you attempt to shop the Internet without a solid foundation of knowledge as to what makes for good value, good quality, and good prices, you are bound to make mistakes and waste money. My intention in this book is to provide the information you will need to use the Internet to buy furniture in the smartest way possible, so that this wonderful new tool will be a pleasure for you to use and not a burden.

Now let's take a look at what's happening on the Internet in the world of furniture and see how you can get ready for it.

According to *The Economist* of November 6, 1999, the ultimate web business would be a site that sells dollar bills for eighty-five cents and makes its money from advertising. What is amazing is that this is almost happening: www.buy.com promises that it has the lowest prices on earth for the products it sells on its site, and that the prices are at or below the cost of the items. What buy.com is hoping is that advertisers who buy space on their site will bring home the bacon. Time will tell.

chapter 1

"Good" and "Bad" Furniture

every week on my web site and in my e-mail (see p. 92 for details), I get the question: "Is Brand X good furniture?" In fact, I get the question so often that I think it is important for us to look at just what "good furniture" and "bad furniture" are. This question comes up with every shopper looking at furniture in brick-and-mortar retail stores, and it will come up even more frequently with shoppers on the Internet because most of the furniture offered for sale on the Internet is, for the most part, "no-name" furniture. You will rarely recognize the furniture brands that you will be thinking about buying (I'll explain why later on in the book). So what is "good furniture" and what is "bad furniture"?

Well, without trying to be too cute, there really is no "bad furniture." There is inexpensive furniture. There is inappropriate furniture. There is poorly constructed furniture. There is over-priced furniture. There is ugly furniture. There is defective furniture. But the term "bad" misses the point and you will miss the point if you don't think this through. "Bad" is such a subjective term that if I do not make myself clear to you when talking about how to be a smart furniture shopper, you will get the message that only expensive furniture is "good" and that definitely is not my message to you.

Chapter 1 Good and Bad Furniture

It would be easy to say that the only "good" furniture is expensive furniture. But this just isn't the case. There are, of course, many details in the construction of both wooden and upholstered furniture. These details, depending on how they are handled, will make some furniture better than others from a quality standpoint. However, the terms "good" and "bad" are best used to describe how well the furniture you are interested in will do a job for you. If you are looking for furniture for your first apartment, or furniture for your son's or daughter's room, or furniture for your summer place at the lake, then modest or inexpensive furniture could be perfect and perfectly "good." Conversely, if you are re-doing your dream house with a substantial budget and you love wonderful things, then buying inexpensive, starter furniture would be a "bad" idea.

In other words, "good" and "bad" relate to the goals you are trying to accomplish. Think of it this way: If you like to tour "off road," buying a Jaguar would be bad. The Jaguar isn't bad, your choice of it for the intended function is bad, and this is how you should evaluate the furniture you are considering purchasing. Whether or not the furniture is a good or a bad buy is a more important consideration, because in every price category some choices are always better than others.

A new entry into the market is the wood furniture being produced in the Far East, Egypt, Spain, and the Philippines. This influx of overseas furniture, produced at dramatically lower prices than is possible by U.S. manufacturers, is making it possible to buy higher quality furniture at prices considerably lower than in the past. Most of this product is "invisible." It is imported by major manufacturers in the U.S. and put into their lines under their own brand names. While this practice does increase the price of the product, it still results in lower prices for wonderfully designed and constructed merchandise. Prices are getting even better and you will be able to buy much more affordable furniture than ever before. Stop worrying about good and bad. Start looking at furniture from this standpoint: Is it a good value? If it isn't a good value, it is bad for you in the context of the problem you are trying to solve.

With all the hype concerning the Internet, it is important to keep perspective. Listen to this: According to the December 20, 1999, issue of *Business Week*, Wal-Mart's total sales for the day after Thanksgiving were $1.3 billion. That's right, $1.3 billion for the day! By contrast, amazon.com's expected sales for the whole year are $1.5 billion. The Internet is big, really big, but it isn't going to kill traditional retailing. Ultimately it is going to make traditional retailing better. More importantly, it is going to put power in the hands of the consumer. That is the really big news. Are you ready for it?

chapter 2

Before You Start Shopping

An article in the *San Francisco Chronicle* dated February 9, 2000, illustrates, inadvertently, how not to shop the internet. This was obviously not the writer's intent, but let me share with you the shopping experience used to demonstrate how wonderful an experience Internet furniture shopping can be.

It seems a woman had been shopping for a sofa in the San Francisco area for months and could not find what she wanted. Keep in mind that the San Francisco area, like all major metro areas, is loaded with furniture stores, department stores, consignment stores, discount outlets, and design shops. After all the frustration of not being able to find the perfect sofa, the woman turned to the Internet after hearing about www.furniture.com, a major Internet store. Not only would she find a great selection of furniture, she would also find low prices and possibly no sales taxes or even shipping charges. Who could resist such a deal? The woman went to the site and ended up buying the sofa she could not find locally.

The article went on to report that while there are drawbacks to shopping on the Internet, and the woman didn't get exactly what she wanted, she still had no regrets. This attitude mystifies me. Is this what smart shopping is all about? Buying something that is not exactly what you want?

Chapter 2 Before You Start Shopping

Let's see what this consumer got. She wanted a gray sofa and the fabric she selected was called "elephant," but what she received was a "little on the mossy-green side." Additionally, the sofa was a lot bigger and a lot higher off the ground than she had expected. Still, it was very comfortable and beautiful and it cost under $800, which the woman considered a "bargain for what appears to be a sofa of decent quality." A happy customer!

It's obvious that this story does not illustrate smart shopping but lucky shopping. I want to take the luck out of shopping, and I can if you are willing to make a small investment of time. To be a smart Internet furniture shopper, you must know what you are doing. It is even more important to know what you are doing when shopping the Internet than it is when you are shopping in your local stores.

The greatest strength of the Internet, and the greatest benefit for all of us, is that the Internet puts at our fingertips at any time of the day or night the whole world of furniture. While the furniture is not necessarily for sale on the Internet (more about that later), at the very least it is for view. No longer are you restricted to a few local stores (or even one local store if you are in a rural area), with a typically small lineup of merchandise. No longer will your imagination be governed by the furniture designs and room settings you see in advertisements and home magazines. In short, the Internet as a shopping tool is the best thing to happen to consumers since the invention of the credit card. The greatest weakness of the Internet is that, while it opens a world of furniture to you from an informational sense, it presents so many choices that you can crash from information overload. Information without understanding can be worse than no information at all. What do I mean by that? To be a smart shopper you must bring to the shopping experience an understanding of not only what you want to accomplish, but also an understanding of what constitutes value and quality. If you don't know the fundamentals of quality and value in furniture you cannot make a good decision. While it's possible to get lucky, the more informed you are, the less you will have to depend on luck to drive the success of your purchases. I am talking about preparation and planning. If you prepare well, and generate a clear idea of what you want to accomplish in the way of price, size, color, style, and lifestyle compatibility, your shopping on the Internet will be time well spent.

Before I go further, I need to explain the different types of Internet furniture sites that you will run into. The first is the virtual furniture store. Virtual stores exist only on the Internet. For example, there are no brick-and-mortar furniture.com stores to visit—anywhere. Virtual stores demand a great leap of faith on your part to go ahead and order furniture that you may not have seen. In fairness it must be noted that some virtual stores, furniture.com for instance, will allow you to return merchandise that you order within a 30-day period and will pay for shipping both ways. This is a fine feature, and it removes much of the apprehension you could have about making a mistake.

The second type of Internet furniture retailer is the Internet store that also has a national network of retail stores. You can shop the Internet site and then go into the local store and physically look at the merchandise. This type of Internet site is maintained by companies such as J. C. Penney, Macys, and Levitz. You can purchase the merchandise on the web site or at the local outlet, whichever proves to be most convenient. This arrangement offers the best of all possible worlds, since you can shop at your leisure and then go into the local store and confirm your decisions after looking at the items that interest you. No longer will you be at the mercy of the salesperson on the floor. It most cases you will be better informed than the salesperson on the floor. This is the best way both to maximize the strengths of the Internet and to avoid making mistakes. In my opinion the combination of Internet store and local store network will prove to be the big winner in retailing for years to come.

The third type of Internet furniture site are the web sites of major national brand manufacturers like La-Z-Boy, Ethan Allen, Drexel-Heritage, and Thomasville, all of which have local, independent, and company-owned showcase stores in many areas. Most of these web sites do not offer the opportunity to buy furniture on the site, but will refer you to your nearest local dealer. Since a large percentage of local stores are independently owned, you will seldom be able to obtain a price quote from the web site. The great advantage of these sites is the ability to shop their lines at your leisure, obtain information, and enter the physical store as an informed consumer. Again you will not be at the mercy of a salesperson who may not know what he or she is talking about. Potentially this type of site has great promise for the buying public because it will enable consumers to shop the best of the American manufacturers' total line of merchandise.

The fourth type of Internet furniture site is the manufacturer's web site that will sell directly to the consumer. This site can be a challenge if you don't know anything about the manufacturer. Is the manufacturer good or bad? Does the furniture represent a real value or not? You will know what the company chooses to tell you about itself on the web site, but how will you judge this information? Incidentally, I will discuss what to look out for in Chapter 5, but suffice it to say that there are real clues that can keep you out of trouble. One of the more promising aspects of this type of web site is that it can and will showcase smaller niche manufacturers and craftsmen who produce exciting furniture. It has been next to impossible for these types of small companies to get floor space in retail stores. They simply don't produce enough furniture, nor do they produce it fast enough for a retailer to give them floor space. But these small companies could be a treasure chest of wonderfully new and exciting merchandise. Give them a look and you may find a real winner.

The fifth and final category of furniture web site is maintained by the brick-and-mortar retail store. Typically, these sites take orders over the Internet for any of its merchandise.

Let me digress for a moment on one of the major pitfalls of the Internet. This is the fact that web sites can make all the players look the same. On the computer screen, all the pictures of furniture, either of poor or high quality, will have much the same appearance. There is just no way to judge the quality of an item by looking at a picture of it, and you certainly cannot compare the quality of two items by looking at pictures. Again, this means you need to be a prepared consumer. Remember, no one is ever going to tell you that you are making a mistake.

Brick-and-Mortar vs. Internet

Let's take a look at some commonly held attitudes about physical furniture stores as compared to virtual furniture stores. Logic suggests that since Internet stores have no physical presence, and thus none of the overhead that "real" stores have, they must be offering better prices. This is true on the one hand but not true on the other. It would be true if the Internet store and the local store carried the same merchandise, but this is rarely the case. Almost without exception, the major furniture manufacturers in the U.S. have restricted the retailers that show their merchandise from offering that merchandise on the Internet. Not only that, many of the most highly recognized brands, such as Century, Drexel-Heritage, Thomasville, and Lexington, even demand that the dealers who elect to show their product not discount that product over 40 percent off of the published Manufacturer's Suggested Retail Price (MSRP). Thus the product that you will be offered on the virtual store's web page is merchandise that is generally not shown in local stores. When you look at the manufacturers on a virtual store's lineup of available merchandise, you will rarely recognize any of them. Is this a problem? Yes and no. It is a problem if you are the typical consumer who needs to see, touch, and experience an item before you buy. Most consumers need to see the product, and it is this fact that has made many of the traditional manufacturers and retailers doubt if virtual furniture retailing on the Internet will be a success.

In 1998, industry sources indicated that furniture purchases on the Internet amounted to $20 million dollars, but that within the next three years sales were expected to exceed $1.4 billion dollars. With this kind of growth expected, you can see there is a wide variance between the attitudes of old-line manufacturers and retailers and those retailers and industry observers who are embracing the world of the Internet. Which group is going to be right? In one sense it doesn't matter, because whatever group is right, the winner is going to be the consumer. Why? Because both the Internet retailer and the traditional brick-and-mortar merchant are going to have to change and accommodate the best of both worlds in order to survive. The merchant in your town will have to change and provide a more exciting, better organized, better staffed, and more consumer-oriented place to shop. The Internet store will have to overcome

Chapter 2 Before You Start Shopping

its lack of a physical presence by making it possible for you to experience the merchandise offered before you buy. The final part of the puzzle is that manufacturers will have to improve shipping times of their products and increase the ability to customize product to the consumer's needs. Is all this possible? Sure it is, and you will be seeing more product, buying it at better prices, and relating to it more than has ever been the case in the past.

At this juncture it's important to realize that I am not talking about "better prices" as the result of increased discounting. We all know that, traditionally, furniture purchases and furniture merchandising have been discount driven. Every week we are bombarded by 40 percent off, 50 percent off, no payments for a year, 2 for 1, no sales tax, and "come to Carolina" ads that promise great savings on brand-name goods. The better prices I am talking about are going to come about by the Internet exposure of hundreds, if not thousands, of heretofore obscure manufactures and retailers. With the availability of increased production from the Far East and the addition of small craft shops tucked away in remote corners of the country, many new competitors will have a showcase for their goods and services. The increased competition for the consumer's interest will force mainline manufacturers and retailers to find ways to be more competitive—or they will be the losers. This is the real strength of the Internet. It will very quickly become the largest marketplace the world has ever known, and consumers will benefit. Will it be trouble-free? No, but this is why smart consumers make the effort to stay informed.

As you begin using your computer to become an "Internet shopper," you will be exposed to a whole new vocabulary. I have included a glossary of the most often used Internet terms for your reference. Remember, if you are having trouble with terms or concepts, feel free to email me or visit my web site (see p. 92).

> Did you know that Network Solutions, the biggest registrar of domain names, has 8.1 million names registered and figures that there are around 11 million names registered worldwide? Network Solutions is registering 15,000 new names a day, or one name every 5 seconds. They predict that within three years there will be 140 million domain names registered. Talk about needing a road map!

Glossary of Internet Terms

ARPAnet: This stands for Advanced Research Projects Agency network, which was the precursor to today's World Wide Web.

Attribute: This defines the way an HTML tag operates. Go to "H" to look up what an HTML is.

Browser: This is an application or computer "roadway" that allows you to navigate the web. The two most popular browsers are Netscape Navigator and Microsoft Internet Explorer.

Bookmark: This is a function of your computer. It could be called "favorites," but whatever it's called, it allows you to establish a direct link to your favorite sites without having to use the search function.

Cookie: This is a string of characters or data that a web site will insert into the cookie file of your browser when you visit a site. This enables the visited site to gather information about how you shopped the site, what links you clicked on and what pages you looked at, and how much time you actually spent at each location. When you come back to that site, it will recognize you and treat you much like a family member returning to the fold. Is it an invasion of privacy? Well, it all depends on what side of the site you are on. (If you like, you can tell the cookie file in your computer program not to accept cookies.)

Domain name: This part of a web site's address can tell you what type of site it is. A ".com" is a commercial site, a ".edu" is an educational site, a ".gov" is a government site, a ".net" is a network site, and, finally a ".org" is the site of some type of organization.

Download: This is an electronic transfer of information from the Internet to your computer's hard drive or a printer.

Double-click: This function means simply that you click the mouse button twice rapidly.

Email: This is electronic mail, a message sent through cyberspace from one person to another.

Encryption: This is a method of scrambling electronic data so that it will not be read by anyone other than the sender and the receiver. It is used in shopping situations most often when dealing with credit card information.

Flame: This is a hostile remark made by one person to another. You shouldn't encounter much of this behavior while shopping. Of course, you may be tempted to flame when you find out the sofa you just ordered is going to take 12 weeks for delivery instead of the promised 4!

Flame war: The above times 10.

Guestbook: This is just what it sounds like. For marketing purposes, the people who maintain web sites want to know as much about you as you will tell them. They will then use this information to alert you about items or programs that you might be interested in. Remember that a considerable amount of information about you will also be collected by cookies—the computer coding devices inserted into your hard drive by web sites (see "cookies"). It is generally your option to allow or not allow this process to happen, but if you opt not to accept a cookie you may not be able to use the site.

Hits: This is the number of results generated when you ask a search engine to find a key word.

Home page: This is every web site's main page.

Hot spot: The mouse cursor will turn into a little hand when it hits a hot spot. This indicates a hyperlink (see hyperlink), which, when clicked, will take you to another site or to another location within the site you are using.

HTML: This stands for "hypertext markup language." Browsers decode this language into text and pictures on your computer screen.

Hyperlink: You will quickly be able to identify hyperlinks because they are underlined and in colored text. When you click on a hyperlink, you will be transported to another but generally related web page. For instance, if you were shopping furniture.com and clicked on one of their featured manufacturer's links, you would go directly to the manufacturer's home page, where you could possibly see more of the furniture you were interested in. To go back, you would click the "back" function and return to the original site. Hyperlinks are tremendously convenient ways to surf the Internet within the category of goods you are investigating.

Hypertext Transfer Protocol (HTTP): If you have a newer browser, you will not have to contend with this. Simply type in the name of the web site under your search function and you will pull up the site. If for any reason this does not get you to the desired site, type http:// in front of, for example, www.furnitureideas.com, and this will tell your computer that you are searching for a site on the World Wide Web and not some other kind of site that does not use HTML.

Icon: This is a small graphic symbol (like the little hand you get on your screen) that represents an application or a command.

Internet: This is the net! Just like the name implies, the internet is a collection of networks that allows computers all over the world to communicate with each other.

Internet Service Provider (ISP): This is a local or national company that provides access to the Internet via your modem.

Modem: This is the device that allows your computer to talk to other computers using your phone line.

QuickTime VR or Virtual Reality: This is very slick software that you can download from the Internet and then plug into your web browser program. It will allow you to circle around a photographed object and even zoom in and out on the picture details. As shopping for furniture becomes more and more sophisticated, you will see more and more of this kind of opportunity presented to you.

Search engine: This is a database of web sites that is linked to certain keywords, like furniture, shopping, or bedding. Lycos, Alta Vista, and Excite are search engines, but there are many more. It is becoming easier to find the addresses of web sites due to increasing media focus and the rise of print and TV advertising that includes web site addresses.

Secure online transaction: This is an Internet transaction in which credit card information is encoded or encrypted so that the seller is the only one who can decipher it. You will be able to tell when you are on a secure site before you give out your credit card number or other sensitive information.

Spam: No, not the canned meat! This is the Internet's term for "junk mail." Specifically, spam is a message that is sent to a multitude of users. Once you begin to use the Internet, you will probably start to get lots of unsolicited e-mail.

Surfing: This is what you do when you click on hyperlinks and go from web site to web site or web page to web page.

Traffic: You will hear Internet advertisements talk about the amount of "traffic" they get on their site. It is simply the amount of visitors to any given page or site.

Uniform Resource Locator (URL): This is the address (such as www.furnitureideas.com), of any given site or page within the site on the web.

UPS (uninterruptable power supply): This is a backup battery supply that allows you to safely shut down your computer if you have a sudden power loss. If I lived in any area of the country that experienced heavy electrical storms, I would certainly have this kind of backup system. Check with any computer hardware store for information on available types.

Web page: This is one element or page within a web site.

Webmaster: This is the person in charge of managing, and often developing, a web site.

World Wide Web: This is the "www" in a web address.

> According to the Forrester Research Group, an Internet research group, it costs from $40 million to $50 million to start an online business in the U.S.
> My web site, www.furnitureideas.com, cost $3,000 to get going, which either means I need to spend a lot more money or the other guys have spent way too much.

Some Helpful Shopping Tips

In its December 10, 1999, issue, *U.S.A. Today* cited a survey by the National Consumers' League that found 50 percent of consumers surveyed believed incorrectly that they had three days to cancel an order after making an on-line purchase. Thirty-three percent believed that web sites are screened (reviewed) before they go up on the Internet. Of course, both these perceptions are incorrect. The Internet is just like any other marketplace in all respects except that it happens to be in your den or office or bedroom. Because it is just like any other collection of stores, it is important for you to be a knowledgeable and careful shopper. Are the chances of being "ripped-off" on the Internet high? Not if you follow these tips:

Make a habit of checking out the Internet retailer before you make a purchase. Look for a reliability seal from bbbonline.com, which is the Internet arm of the Better Business Bureau. Check if *Consumer Reports* has evaluated the site. Go to bizrate.com to see if they have an evaluation of the site. Gomez.com is the best reporting service that I know of. It has extensive evaluations on Internet furniture retailers, which will give you a great deal of helpful information. I wouldn't shop on line without Gomez.com beside me. Finally, you can always e-mail me at lewin@foothill.net.

Do these checks mean you will never have a problem with an Internet retail furniture purchase? Unfortunately, no, but it certainly will help if you keep it all in mind. Frankly, I don't know of any Internet furniture retailer who is lying in wait to rip you off. However, you can easily rip yourself off if you don't do your homework and if you are not prepared with a good plan and a good understanding of just what makes furniture a good or bad value.

Get all your questions answered before you buy anything. Is the item in stock? What is the shipping date? Does the Internet retailer have an "online privacy policy"? Will you get a fabric sample for approval before the order is processed? What is the Internet retailer's return policy? How do you handle a complaint? What if the shipment is delayed? What happens if the shipment is damaged? If you don't get specific and clear answers to all your questions or if the customer service response is slow or poor, take away your business. There are too many Internet furniture retailers for you to feel you are trapped with any one of them. Be selective. Be tough.

Keep very accurate records of everything you purchase. Make a printout of all your records and have the company send you email confirmation of every detail that is important to you and the transaction. Don't rely on verbal promises. If something is not written down and confirmed, it doesn't count. Get confirmation of specific ship dates. Do not rely on comments like, "Well, we expect it to ship in 6 weeks." Be specific and you will be in control.

Give out only basic information. If you are using your credit card to pay for the purchase, and you should (more about this next), you will need to list a ship-to address, your name, address, and phone number and not a whole lot more. If any site wants your social security number or your mother's maiden name, be concerned. Remember, your credit card company has all your information and will okay the transaction. The Internet merchant doesn't need anything but basic information.

> According to Internet survey sources, 52 percent of consumers polled use the Internet to shop because they can avoid crowds! Fifty-one percent say it saves them time, and 41 percent think they are getting better prices.

Always pay with a credit card. This is true even if you are doing business with a local merchant. You, of course, want to be doing business with an Internet retailer who has a secure site—you can tell by looking for a "padlock" or "unbroken key" icon at the bottom of the home page. Also, web site addresses that start with "https://" are secure, but bottom-line: Ask for and receive confirmation from the Internet merchant that the site is secure. When in doubt contact www.bbbonline.com for information.

It is very important to keep these basics in mind. If at any time you feel that you have been badly handled or have any complaint, you can contact the Better Business Bureau at www.bbb.org/complaints. It is also important to realize that you can file a complaint against the offending company with the Federal Trade Commission at www.ftc.gov/ftc/complaint.htm. Everyone from government to industry is eager to make sure the Internet is safe, secure, and satisfactory. You can help make it so by being concerned enough to let everyone know you are not happy with how you were handled.

chapter 3

Shopping for Upholstered Furniture

Upholstery is the most "intimate" of the home furnishings products since it must "fit" you. I didn't say appeal to you, which it also must do, but rather it must "fit" you in a physical sense. Now if you are of average height and weight, most upholstered items will fit you. Remember, I said "most," but certainly not all items. There are potential problems with an item being too deep or too shallow (front to back), having too much pitch (the vertical position either forward or backward), or having arms that are too high for your comfort. All of the foregoing is also compounded by your selection of a fabric type. To help keep you out of trouble, I am going to give you a few key points to keep in mind when buying upholstery on the Internet.

Whenever possible, sit in an upholstered item before you buy it. But wait a minute! How can you sit on Internet furniture? Yes, you guessed it, this will always be a problem with Internet shopping. You will either bring to the buying situation advance knowledge based on years of exposure to advertising (cars, watches, sporting goods, etc.), or your experience with similar product in the past. But interestingly, very few consumers have any real knowledge about furniture as a product or as a brand. Most knowledge about furniture is economic. When we set up our first apartments, we buy a sofa and a pair of chairs for $699, a bed and mattress for $499, a few lamps for $119, take our parents' extra chest for the bedroom, and pay $49 for a stand for the TV and $499 for a kitchen/dining setup. When the children begin to come, we add basics to our furniture collections. With

Chapter 3 Shopping for Upholstered Furniture

the first big promotion, we begin to think about interior design. With our first house, we really begin to think about interior design, but throughout this progression of need and lifestyle changes we rarely accumulate any real knowledge—beyond cost—of the furniture objects we live with. Compounding this approach is the furniture industry's almost total dependence on discount advertising. All the industry ever tells us is that this sofa or that dining room is now 30 percent or 40 percent off! No wonder we don't know anything about furniture except that it is discounted, and this fact is the least important aspect in buying anything. Why? Because you never really learn anything about the product itself and it is knowledge, product knowledge, that allows you to make good choices between competing products that may save you far more money than a discount from a highly inflated suggested retail price list. Think about it. If I could get you a 70 percent discount off RiverLane Plantation Furniture, would it be a good deal? Just to give you something to think about: Wouldn't you want to know more about the furniture itself before the 70 percent discount came into play? Don't buy discounts! They don't mean anything until you have done a lot of research.

Fabric selection can be both the most fun and the most problematic task in selecting upholstered furniture: Fun because the fabric sets the tone of a room, but nerve-racking because most wear problems are a result of your selection. One of the most asked questions I get is "do you think this fabric will wear well"? This can be a tough question to answer because it is so dependent on how the item will be used and by whom. I have had upholstery items that looked good after 20 years of wear and I have had others that looked shopworn after three years. The color of a fabric, the fiber, the way the fabric is woven, and the use it gets all matter tremendously in how the fabric will perform. Most consumers create their own problems by not planning well and by not taking into consideration their lifestyle demands when selecting upholstery fabric. It is all well and good to crave a wonderful white silk sofa, but if your family is still knee deep in Saturday soccer, and the Cub Scouts meet at your house every Thursday, and your husband likes to work on model airplanes in the living room, you should be honest with yourself. That white silk sofa will look like a French battle flag within two months. A good, honest evaluation of your real lifestyle needs will save you money and grief. Keep the following factors in mind also.

Expensive fabrics do not necessarily guarantee durability. Cost really has nothing to do with how much or what kind of wear the fabric will give you. In fact, there is almost an inverse relationship between the cost of a fabric and its wearability. As a rule of thumb, the more expensive the fabric, the more wear problems you will probably encounter. Expense is most often added as a result of elaborate designs and high-quality fibers. Costly weaving and printing processes also add dramatically to fabric cost. Another critical factor in the cost of a fabric is how much waste is involved in cutting the upholstery patterns. There are fabrics that have waste factors of up to 50 percent, believe it or not. This wasted material is added to the cost you will pay for putting that fabric on a sofa or chair.

Keep in mind that none of these factors affect how a fabric will wear. Not one of them. Manufacturers who are trying to sell upholstery at lower prices simply do not include fancy fabrics in their offerings. As a practical matter, I don't expect that you will be given too many fabric choices when you are shopping for upholstery on the Internet. Ordering upholstery in a custom fabric or one different than the fabric shown on the site or floor can result in delivery times of up to 16 weeks. Since most Internet merchants try to offer shipping within 30 days, they have to limit the number of fabrics an item can be ordered in. This isn't a real problem, since most stores and manufacturers offer too many fabrics anyway. If you are working with a designer and have a huge budget, then wading through thousands of fabrics has some merit.

What does affect fabric wear is the type of fiber, how closely woven it is, and, above all, how it will be used. As obvious as this sounds, you and your family will be the biggest factor in determining how well a fabric will wear. This is why it is so important to think through how you actually live in your house. Pets, committee meetings, hobbies, and housecleaning habits all add up and affect everything in your home, particularly the fabrics. If you have a rough-and-tumble group, think about fabrics having a high synthetic fiber count. If you tend to use up the items in your home, consider thinking of your upholstery as temporary—perhaps the solution is to buy modestly priced items that you can replace every several years. Here's the bottom line: Being a smart shopper means being honest with yourself about how items will be used and then buying accordingly. If you do this, you will spend your money more wisely and have fewer gray hairs. Incidentally, I have included for quick reference a glossary of fabric types to use when you are considering fabric selections.

I want to take a moment and talk about leather. Leather is an important part of the upholstery world and it is very big business today. It is selling very well for a lot of reasons, primarily because it is more affordable than ever. Leathers are also better looking than ever. So what's the problem? The problem is that with today's new leathers, some of the old truisms of leather have changed—for better and worse.

To begin with, leather is the longest wearing of any furniture covering, and today's leathers are more varied and beautiful than ever. But ironically, in some cases, today's leather has become more fragile. I don't mean it is going to wear out. Good leather will not wear out but, being a natural product, it will change and develop character. Now character to some people means patina, but to other people it means damage. When you get into today's leathers, you really have to decide what kind of person you are. Are you a "patina" type or are you a "damage" type?

What has changed dramatically is the way leathers are dyed and finished. In the days of yore, leather was routinely finished with a heavy pigmented finish. This finish, often called a London glaze, was thick and slick. It was stiff and over years of use would develop a series of tiny hairline cracks in the finish. Leather "nuts," of which I am one, loved the look of old, cracked leathers, thinking back over the many books discovered in the arms of a great leather chair and the wonderful cigars with just a few whiskeys to while away the hours. Heavens, I want to be in one now! Leathers today are dyed and finished differently, but more about that later.

Once relegated to the den and office, leather today is being used everywhere from the living room to the bedroom and rightly so. When you are shopping in your local stores or the Internet, it is easy to be confused by the wide range of leather offerings. The confusion is the result of both the wonderful new range of leathers and a totally new selection of affordable leather furniture.

The Italians brought affordable leather to the marketplace. Now everyone is into leather—from China to the U.S. You will see good-looking leather sofas offered from $900 and up. What you won't get at this entry-level price range is wonderful construction, and the product will be more "disposable" than the industry standard, which has typically considered good leather as wearing four times as long as the best-wearing fabric. This may be perfectly fine with you, particularly if you are setting up your first home or if the item (and price tag) meet your needs at the time you are shopping. However, it's important that you realize that $900 leather sofas are not the benchmark for the industry. Good leathers are almost indestructible, and it is still a fact that if you are considering leather as a long-time investment in comfort and style, you will have to spend more than $1800 to get it.

On a more practical note, today's leathers are finished with aniline dyes and are often left unprotected. Thus they can be prone to fading, soiling, and marking. Recognizing this, some designers have made a fortune selling "distressed" leather. This leather can be wondrous to the touch and a joy to live with if you are not paranoid about your leather changing almost before your eyes—it may end up looking like an old catcher's mitt. What is the message with leather? Enjoy it. It has never been more beautiful and it has never been as affordable.

I have included a glossary of leather terms to make your shopping easier. Now go out there and buy a leather chair or sofa. You will love it.

Now let's get back to fabric upholstery. Before deciding on a fabric, request a sample. This may sound routine, and it should be routine, but routine or not, request that sample before you order anything. Never be in such a hurry that you fail to do this. Consider the fact that even though you looked at a picture of the item that you are considering ordering in the fabric that you liked, to get an accurate depiction you will be relying on the color correctness of your electronic equipment, which in turn is relying on the color correctness of the web site's equipment. Wow! There is too much faith in technology here to be safe. Another reason to get that sample is that you want to feel the fabric. Does it have a nice "hand"? Does it look like it will withstand wear? Is it tightly woven? What is it made from? All of these factors will contribute not only to the wear but also to the feel and maintenance requirements of the fabric.

Chapter 3 Shopping for Upholstered Furniture

A final note on fabric: Always have the sofa or chair that you purchase treated with a soil protection product. There are several treatments available, but whatever the product offered, buy it. These treatments will cost you an additional $100 to $150 and are worth every cent. Can you protect the fabric yourself with a spray can from the local hardware store? You sure can, and remember, you could also take out your own appendix it you wanted to. Trust me: Buy the service. It should also come with an extended warranty that will protect you down the road. But as is the case with everything you are considering buying, check the fine print and get a copy of the warranty for your records. If the site you are considering does not offer fabric protection as an option, I would pass them by. This is a basic necessity that I think is too important to pass up, and if it isn't offered, I would be nervous about the company.

When buying upholstered furniture, the construction features you should ask about—and look for—are a sturdy kiln-dried hardwood frame that is glued, screwed, and corner-blocked. An upholstered item that doesn't have a state-of-the-art frame cannot and will not give good long-term service. With this necessary solid foundation, your next consideration is the type of "spring-deck" the item has. An 8-way, hand-tied spring-up system is the benchmark of quality in the industry, but it is certainly no guarantee of top quality. It is, though, an indication of better quality. Other spring-up systems can be more than adequate: "z-springs," drop-in 8-way systems, rubber web-based systems, etc.

Here is a short list of the essential elements to keep in mind when considering any upholstery item:

Frame: The most basic element and the foundation of any upholstery item, expensive or inexpensive, is the frame: If the item doesn't have a good frame, it is not going to do the job for you. A good frame will be constructed of kiln-dried hardwood. It will be assembled under pressure and each corner assembly will be glued, screwed, double-doweled and corner-blocked. The front legs will be a corner-blocked assembly that is glued, screwed, and double-doweled into the front corners of the frame. The back legs will be the lower extension of the vertical back rail that runs to the top of the frame's back rail, which is also corner-blocked, glued, and screwed into the frame.

Wood: All wood should be free of knots and should be at least 1 inch in diameter. You should never accept any screw-on leg assemblies with the one exception being on long sofas, over 90 inches in length, where you may see a screw-on leg positioned in the center of the sofa to support the long run of rails and springs. This is not only okay, it is something to look for in better sofas. Longer sofas will often have a decorative center leg that is doweled and blocked into the front center rail.

Base: This is the area to which the springs are attached. On the very best upholstery items, this will be a series of woven straps that in today's world are most often polypropylene. On this base the springs rest and are clipped to the base and then tied 8 ways to each other and to the base rails. This is the 8-way, hand-tied spring base/deck. When done right, this is the best construction. Sinuous wire spring decks are certainly acceptable, as are drop-in 8-way spring systems, but it is important to remember that anything other than the 8-way hand-tied system is, while acceptable, of lesser quality and the item should be priced accordingly.

Cushions: Good cushions do not make up for a bad deck, but with that proviso in mind, the standard cushion used by most manufacturers is a variation of a polyurethane foam core wrapped with polyester fiberfill. The core can be either HR (High Resiliency) foam, which is the best, or HC (High Comfort) foam, used in better products. Remember that it is all right to buy almost any product if it fits your needs and if the price is appropriate for what you are getting. Often you will have the option of selecting all down, or poly-down, or spring-down cushions. In almost all cases these choices will increase the price of the upholstery item. Will they be superior to the standard cushion? Not necessarily. In almost all cases, combination-down or all-down cushions make for a softer cushion with less "recovery" than poly cushions. If you like the softer seat and the more relaxed look, then by all means go with down or combination down.

Pillows: The manufacturing standard for pillow fillings is polyester fiberfill. On better products you will generally have an option of using down or a combination down filling at increased cost. The considerations are the same as with cushions, as these options give a softer, more relaxed look. If you are offered a down or combination-down cushion and pillow option as a standard feature, you may have a real value on your hands, but never feel you are being slighted if the standard is a well done polyester-wrapped polyurethane core.

Padding: All better upholstery has padding that covers the wooden parts of the frame. In fact, padding should be under the outer upholstery cover in all areas, not only to cover the wooden members, but also to flesh out the arm and back panels so that there are no spots where fabric stretches over open space. Anytime fabric is stretched over an unpadded wooden member, the wear on the fabric at that spot will be greatly increased. Inexpensive upholstery is generally very poorly padded. This doesn't mean you shouldn't buy it, but it does mean that your expectations should not be too high and you shouldn't pay too much for the item.

All other considerations—tight-back or loose-pillow back, skirted or unskirted, tight-seat or cushioned, high-arm or low-arm, three- or two-cushion—are ones of personal preference.

> Always ask what the Joint Industry Upholstery Standards Committee Cleaning Code designation is for any fabric that you are considering purchasing. It will help you to take proper care of the fabric. The more you know about the items you are considering purchasing, the happier you will be with your elections.

The Care and Cleaning of Upholstery

Once you have purchased the upholstery of your dreams (or wallet), you must take care of it. Keeping upholstery clean is more of a challenge than keeping wood furniture in good shape, but it shouldn't be a major chore. I hope you take my advice and have your new upholstery treated with soil-repellant. This is a definite "must have" in my book, well worth the money.

Your main concern with upholstery is to keep it as dust-free as possible and to make sure the deck area (under the cushions) is kept free of crumbs, dirt, and foreign matter. If you can remember to rotate and reverse your cushions and pillows every two weeks, do so. This will even out the wear on the upholstery and extend its life. The areas most prone to dirt buildup are the lengths of the arms, with the front ends of the arms getting the most wear. Arm caps, which some manufacturers enclose with the item as a matter of course, are always a good idea. If you don't get arm caps, buy an extra yard of fabric and have arm caps made for you locally. Keeping your upholstery as clean and dust-free as possible is the most you can do yourself.

Chapter 3 Shopping for Upholstered Furniture

You should never try to spot-clean upholstery, since you could very easily end up with a lighter area that is as noticeable as a dirty area. Always have your upholstery cleaned by a professional. A final word on any cleaning program is to know what the recommended cleaning program is for the upholstery fabric. The Joint Industry Upholstery Standards Committee has come up with cleaning standards for all upholstery fabrics. Most manufacturers label their fabrics with the recommended cleaning code. Anytime you are buying an upholstered item, the retailer will be able to tell you about the recommended cleaning code. If the store (be it on the Internet or down the street) can't tell you what the cleaning code is, I wouldn't spend my money there. Any well-run retailer has this information available to them. Here are the Code designations and what they stand for:

"W" Remove soil with the foam of a water-based cleaning agent. Many household cleaning solvents are harmful to the color and life of a fabric. Dry cleaning by a professional furniture cleaning service only is recommended. To prevent overall soil, remove dust and grime by frequent vacuuming or light brushing.

"WS" Clean the fabric with shampoo, foam, or dry cleaning solvents as desired. Do not saturate with liquid. Pile fabrics may require brushing to restore appearance. Cushion covers should not be removed and dry-cleaned.

"S" Clean the fabric with pure solvents (petroleum distillate-based products) in a well-ventilated room. The use of water-based or detergent-based solvent cleaners may cause excessive shrinking. Water stains may be impossible to remove with solvent cleaning agents. Avoid products containing carbon tetrachloride, as it is highly toxic. Remove dust and grime by frequent vacuuming or light brushing. Dry cleaning by a professional furniture cleaning service only is recommended.

"SW" Clean the fabric with a water-based cleaning agent or with a pure solvent in a well-ventilated room (petroleum distillate-based products). Dry cleaning by a professional furniture cleaning service only is recommended. Remove dust and grime by frequent vacuuming or light brushing.

"X" Clean the fabric by vacuuming or light brushing. Water-based foam or solvent-based cleaning agents of any kind may cause excessive shrinking or fading.

Glossary of Fabrics and Fabric Facts

Applique: This is a pattern of a fabric that is cut out, then sewed or pasted onto the surface of another fabric.

Batik: The pattern of a fabric is covered with wax and then dyed. The wax is removed after dyeing, producing a white pattern on the dyed background. This process is repeated to make multicolored designs.

Boucle: Woven or knit fabric whose surface is looped or knotted. This term is derived from the French word meaning "curled" or "buckled."

Brocade: A class of rich, heavy, jacquard-woven fabrics with raised floral or figured patterns. The look is emphasized by contrasting surfaces or colors.

Brocatelle: Similar to brocade, but with designs that are in high relief. It is made on a jacquard loom with a satin or twill figure on a plain or satin background. The pattern has a distinctive blistered or puffed appearance.

Calender: A process in which cloth is pressed to produce a smooth, glossy, or other special finish.

Calico: A term that was formerly used to describe a plain, woven, printed cotton cloth similar to percale. The name is taken from Calicut, India, where it was first produced.

Cambric: A plain-weave soft cotton or linen fabric calendered with a slight luster on the face.

Canvas: A general classification of strong, firm, closely woven fabrics that usually are made from cotton.

Cashmere: A soft wool textile made from Indian goat hair. The same breed of goat is now found in the U.S., Europe, and South America.

Chenille: A type of woven yarn, which has a pile projecting all around at right angles to the body thread. Think of your bath towel!

Chiffon: A sheer, gauze-like, silk fabric.

Chintz: A glazed, plain-weave cotton fabric decorated with brilliantly colored figures, flowers, etc. A major upholstery fabric, common on Early American pieces.

Chapter 3 Shopping for Upholstered Furniture 35

Corduroy: A strong, durable fabric with a cotton ground and vertical cut pile "stripes" formed by an extra row of filling yarns.

Crewel: Embroidery using wool worked on unbleached cotton or linen. It was widely used during the Jacobean Period for upholstery and drapes and, more recently, during the 1960s and 1970s for use on wing chairs. Crewel has a wonderful look that should be used more often in today's traditional homes.

Damask: A broad group of jacquard-woven fabrics having elaborate floral or geometric patterns, generally made from linen, cotton, wool, silk, rayon, etc. The pattern is distinguished from the ground by a contrasting luster. A damask fabric is reversible.

Denim: A heavy cotton cloth of a twill weave.

Duck: A canvas-like material often given a protective finish against fire, water, etc. Early rainwear manufacturers used this material for their garments.

Embroidery: The art of decorating a material with needle and thread. It is thought to have originated in Italy during the 16th Century, probably to give ladies of leisure something to do!

Felt: This is material made by matting together, under heat and pressure, woolen fibers or cowhair, etc.

Fiberglass: This is a trade name for a fabric woven from fine filaments of glass. It is sometimes used for automobile bodies, has great strength, and resists heat, chemicals, and soil. It can be quite soft and pliable and made into a cloth.

Flannel: This can be wool or cotton fabric of coarse soft yarns that are "napped." This means that the ends of the yarn are loosened during the production of this soft clothing and bed-sheet material. You may see it used as an upholstery material.

Frise: Pronounced "free-zay," this is a pile fabric with uncut loops. It can be produced using most materials and is very durable. You may have seen it on lobby sofas in old movie houses. It is usually produced in nylon for commercial use.

Gabardine: Hard-finished twill not often used for upholstery fabrics. It is firm and durable.

Gingham: Lightweight yarn-dyed cotton material, usually woven in checks or stripes.

Hand: An industry/trade term used to describe how a fabric "feels." Velvet can have a wonderful hand. Sailcloth generally has a poor hand.

Homespun: A term used to describe hand-loomed woolen textiles. The look can also be produced on power looms.

Jacquard Weaves: Perhaps the most utilized weave pattern to produce upholstery fabrics, including brocades, tapestry, matelasse, damasks, and jacquard velvet fabrics.

Khaki: A heavy cotton-twill fabric, traditionally an earth-brown color. The word now describes both the fabric and the color. It was first produced in India as a tough material for English military uniforms. In the 1950s it was worn every day by eastern schoolboys as the pants of choice.

Lace: An openwork textile produced by needle, pin, or bobbin, using the process of sewing, knitting, or crocheting. Lace was first made in Greece, but then spread to most European countries as a cottage industry. Real lace is a handmade product seldom seen in the marketplace because so few craftspeople make it these days. Lace, of course, can be made on power looms.

Leno: This is a type of weave that results in a fabric with a netlike appearance. You will seldom see this weave. Perhaps Jay Leno would like to invite me onto his show to discuss it more fully?

Matelasse: A double or compound fabric with a quilted character and raised patterns that create a puckered or pocketed effect. It is a significant upholstery fabric with most of its appeal in the South and East. Generally quite expensive.

Mohair: This is yarn and cloth made from the fleece of the Angora goat. The fiber is wiry and strong, making mohair one of the most durable of all fabrics. It had a great surge of popularity during the late 1950s as the sweater material all young ladies had to have. Interestingly, I am beginning to see a resurgence of these sweaters on the avenues.

Moiré: This is a finish process that produces a watermarked appearance on silk or cotton fabric.

Chapter 3 Shopping for Upholstered Furniture

Muslin: A plain, woven, white cotton fabric that can be bleached or left unbleached. Its principal use in furniture has been as a base cover on upholstered items before the outer upholstery was applied. Double upholstery is seldom done any more, in the interest of reducing manufacturing costs, but it was a common practice with higher-end manufacturers as late as the 1970s.

Needlepoint: An old-fashioned cross-stitch done on net, heavy canvas, or linen. This embroidery technique, along with lace making, is seldom practiced by hand any more. The needlepoint effect can be produced on power looms and is seen only on a limited basis in furniture showrooms today.

Nylon: One of the great inventions of the modern world. This material is a wonder of chemistry. It is tough, elastic, and very flexible in its applications. It is often used today in textiles where silk and rayon were the previous fibers of choice.

Paisley: A printed or woven design in the imitation of original Scotch shawl patterns made in the town of Paisley, Scotland.

Percale: A plain, closely woven muslin fabric in a dull finish, which may be bleached, dyed, or printed. It is very similar to chintz.

Pile fabrics: The velvets, friezes, and most plush types. These fabrics are used on both traditional and contemporary upholstery items.

Plush: A fabric with a long pile, made of silk, wool, cotton, or a synthetic fiber. It is made like velvet and the nap is sometimes pressed down to form a surface resembling fur.

Plain weaves: These are the satins, taffetas, and sateens done in a finer thread count. The coarser weaves are often used in both contemporary and colonial settings.

Poplin: A durable, plain weave class of fabrics made of silk, cotton, wool, synthetics, or any combination of these fabrics.

Printed Fabrics: Most often cottons, both glazed and unglazed. You will also see printed linen. Heavily used as draperies, but also for upholstery, having much appeal in colonial/early American themes. Often quilted, printed fabrics offer a great range of colors and patterns.

Quilted Fabric: This is a double fabric with padding between the layers that is held in place by stitching that is usually done in a pattern. This is still a big part of today's decorating/design environment, particularly in the East and South. It is less utilized in the West, but when used adds a lovely touch to a traditional room setting. Bear in mind that quilting adds greatly to an item's cost. With this in mind, the technique called "combination quilt" is used: The inside areas of a sofa or chair are upholstered, as are the cushions and pillows, with the quilted fabric, while the outside arms, back, and sides use the same, but unquilted, fabric. This approach can result in a significant cost reduction without detracting from the look you are trying to achieve.

Rayon: Another wonder of the chemical lab. Rayon is more lustrous, stiffer, and less expensive than silk. In combination with silk, wool, or cotton, its possibilities are limitless.

Rep: A plain-weave fabric made with a heavy filler thread that gives a corded effect. Rep is unpatterned and reversible, and can be made using any fiber.

Sailcloth: Similar to canvas. It is very durable and often used for summer furniture.

Sateen: A strong, lustrous, cotton fabric with a smooth surface.

Satin: A smooth, generally lustrous, fabric, with a thick, close texture, made of silk. The fibers can be manmade or natural done in a satin weave.

Strie: This is a fabric with a narrow streak or striped effect that is almost the same color as the background. The term "striated" is used to describe the striped effect on any fabric.

Synthetic fibers: Rayon, Celanese, Dacron, Fortisan, Lurex, Orlon, and Herculon all can be used on their own to produce fabrics, or in combination with natural fibers to produce wonderful new looks and textures. Few inventions of modern chemistry have had more impact on modern society than these products.

Taffeta: A fabric woven in a basic plain weave, usually made of silk, with warp and weft threads of equal size. You will find taffeta made from several synthetic fibers also.

Chapter 3 Shopping for Upholstered Furniture

Tapestry: This is a heavy hand- or machine-woven fabric with decorative designs that usually depict historical scenes. The pattern appears on both sides of the fabric with the difference being, on the backside, that the loose thread ends are visible. Tapestries were first used as wall coverings to honor great events of the age or to depict classical themes. Many surviving hand-made tapestries from the 17th and 18th centuries are true works of art. Today's upholstery tapestry is generally rugged-wearing and a beautiful choice for key items. Done in synthetic fibers, they can even be most affordable.

Textured Weaves: These are generally copies of hand-woven fabrics and are frequently used in upholstery and draperies.

Tweed: A class of rough wool fabrics with a wiry, somewhat hairy surface, but having a soft, flexible texture. The weave may be plain, twill, herringbone, or a novelty. These are generally thought of as Scottish weaves, but they are not necessarily limited to Scotland. However, if you are involved in a wager about the source of tweed, always pick Scotland. You will be right more often than wrong.

Velour: This is a general term for any fabric that resembles velvet. Velour is the French term for velvet—remember that if you are looking for a velvet sofa in Paris!

Velvet: This is a fabric that has a thick, short pile on the surface and a plain back. It is usually made by weaving the fabric face to face, and then slicing the fabric in two. Velvets can be cotton, linen, silk, synthetic, or any combination of the fibers listed.

Velveteen: This fabric is woven and then the loops are sheared to produce the fine close pile. It is sometimes called cotton velvet even though it is not woven face to face, as are true velvets. This is a less complicated process than the necessary slicing operation of true velvets and generally less costly.

Vinyl: This is a textile that has been fused or coated with vinyl plastic. It was first mass-produced in 1939. The surface can be printed or embossed. It is often used in the furniture world in combination with leathers or as an inexpensive substitute for leather. Don't turn your nose up at this versatile product. It can offer a nice, inexpensive solution to many home decorating problems.

Glossary of Synthetic Fabrics

Acetate: Acele, Avisco, Celanese, Chromspun, and Estron are trade names for this economical upholstery fabric fiber. It is not very good used alone and most often will be blended with other fibers either natural or synthetic. Acetate does have a tendency to fade in heavy sunlight.

Acrylic: Acrilan, Cresian, Orlon, and Zefran are trade names for this fiber, which is often used to produce wool-like fabrics. Acrylic cleans up well and is finding increasing applications in upholstery fabrics.

Modacrylic: Dynel and Verel are trade names for this fiber, which is similar to acrylic. It is even more soil-resistant than acrylic, and can be used to great advantage when creating fur-like fabrics. You will see modacrylic most often in the home as faux (fake) fur throws and rugs. (By the way, modacrylic rugs and throws are fire-retardant if you want to have one in front of your fireplace for those winter evenings, but remember, fire-retardant does not mean fireproof.)

Nylon: A.C.E., Antron, and Cordura are trade names for this granddaddy of the synthetics. Nylon can have a silk-like texture and is often blended with other fibers to create wonderful fabrics. It does have a tendency to fade in sunlight but it is widely used in carpeting.

Olefin (polypropylene): Herculon and Vectra are trade names of this widely used upholstery fiber. Though economical and soil-resistant, it presents a problem in strong sunlight. Olefin is never used in formal settings—it is a more casual look, often woven into plaids. Olefin is an excellent choice when you are looking for economy and tough wear.

Polyester: Dacron, Fortrel, and Trevira are trade names for this workhorse of the furniture industry. It is widely used for cushion fillings (it is today's substitute for down). It can have either a silk or wool-like hand.

Rayon: Avril, Enka, and Zantrel are trade names of this synthetic, which is another economical substitute for silk and cotton. Most often used as a blend with other fibers to produce upholstery fabrics. It is made from cellulose, which occurs naturally in plants.

Triacetate: Arnel is the trade name of this fiber, which is seldom, if ever, used for upholstery fabrics. I included it because you will see it when you look at drapery fabrics for your home.

Plastics

Vinyl: Naugahyde is the trade name for this widely used leather substitute. Vinyl unfairly gets a bum rap, considering it offers so much economy and is quite decent looking. When the need is there, it is tough to beat this material. It's great for dinette seats and commercial uses, easy to clean, and available in a multitude of colors. In all fairness it is not a good substitute for leather because it does not offer the durability, feel, or smell of leather. You will see vinyl used in conjunction with leather by manufacturers who are offering "leather-mate" items. These are upholstery items that use leather on the inside areas of the sofa or chair, but then use vinyl on the outside back and arms of the item. Properly color-matched, this is a legitimate way to greatly reduce retail price and bring sofas and chairs to a great many consumers who simply can't afford an all-leather item.

> Relatively recent innovations in vinyl production have introduced perforated "poromerics," which are vinyls that "breathe" like natural leather. These will never, of course, replace leather as the covering of choice, but perfected they will eliminate one of vinyl's big drawbacks, which is the fact that it sticks to you. Many of us can attest to the fact that getting up after an hour on a vinyl sofa can be an uncomfortable experience for bare skin.

Glossary of Leather Terms

Aniline: This is a transparent dye used to color leather all the way through. It is considered transparent because it doesn't cover or conceal range marks or the natural graining of the leather.

Pure aniline: This is a tricky term that sounds like something special, and it is special in that it can give you special problems. What "pure aniline" really means is that the leather has been colored with an aniline dye but has no protective finish.

Semi-aniline: Other terms for semi-aniline are aniline-plus or protected aniline. This refers to a piece of leather that is aniline-dyed and then coated with a matching pigment to even out the color and to provide some protection.

Antique/distressed: These terms apply any time leather has been mechanically given additional marks to simulate natural aging and wear.

Corrected grain: Leather that has been buffed to remove undesirable blemishes and embossed (a pattern pressed under pressure into the leather) to simulate an attractive grain (like crocodile) or other decorative texture.

Full grain: Top-grain leather with no corrections or alterations to the natural grain pattern. Not often seen except on very high-end products. "Full grain" is used in Europe interchangeably with the term "top grain." Unfortunately, neither "full grain" nor "top grain" guarantees that you are getting the best leather possible. Ponder the fact that even "top grain" from a sick animal will just not be that good. As always, shop cautiously.

Leather-vinyl combinations: This is an upholstering technique where the manufacturer will use leather on the inside areas and cushions/pillows but will then put a color-coordinated vinyl on the outside arms and back. Terms like "leather-mate" are used to describe this approach. This method of construction saves production costs and, when done well, looks good.

Natural markings or range marks: These are markings on leather that are common on animals that have been out roaming the range. They are marks made by barbed wire, scratches, brand marks, insect bites, and stretch marks—all of the common marks that result from animals roaming freely. Incidentally, all of these marks can be simulated by mechanical means.

Nubuck: This is top-grain, aniline-dyed leather that has been buffed to create a soft nap. Nubuck is wonderful but very vulnerable to stains, so it is often lightly finished to offer some protection. Nubuck is usually quite expensive and looks like suede but it isn't: Suede is made from a split hide so it is not as grand a leather as Nubuck.

Patina: This term describes that luster or shine that develops with use over time. It is often used to describe the wonderful glow that fine old wood furniture and other antiques acquire over the years. Fussy customers and the unsophisticated work hard for the clean look that only plastic can offer day to day. Relax, and use your fine things. Care for them, but use them, and years from now someone will remark on the wonderful patina an item of yours has acquired. I have this term under leather because the new, wonderful leathers are on the one hand very tough while on the other hand very prone to developing a "patina" (read soiling).

Chapter 3 Shopping for Upholstered Furniture

Pigmented leather: This leather has been finished with a solid-pigment coating to achieve consistent color and texture. The more pigment used, the "stiffer" the leather becomes, but the process protects the leather from everyday soil, spills, etc. Pigmented leather has been used for years and could be described as the "classic" look for chairs and sofas. It can have either a high-gloss or mat finish. Over the years, a high-gloss finish will develop a spider web of tiny cracks—these add character to the leather and in no way harm it. Where tough wear and durability are desired, pigmented leather could be the best choice.

Pull-up: This is a full-grain, aniline-dyed leather that is waxed or oiled. It has a rich, somewhat oily hand (feel); the oil won't rub off on clothes, but gives the leather a wonderful feeling of "life." This finish is generally found at the high-end of the leather market.

Sauvage: This is a visual effect that produces a mottled, or tone-on-tone, look. It is a technique used to add character or depth to leather.

Split: This is the bottom layer of a hide that has been "split-off" from the top grain. It can be made into suede or finished to resemble top-grain hides. Any time you see leather prices that are too good to be true, you may be looking at a spit hide. Is it bad? No, just don't pay too much money for it.

Top coat: This is a transparent protective coating applied to the leather surface.

Top grain: This is the best leather, but the term has become blurry since top grain and full grain are often used interchangeably. Some suppliers and manufacturers use the term full grain to indicate an uncorrected top cut of the leather, while others use the term top grain to mean the same thing. Whichever term is used, it will be used to denote the best cut of the hide. It should be the uppermost layer of the hide—the outer surface. This is what you want, but be careful, there are a lot of "top grains" that should have been buried with the animal. Think about this: You will see "Top-Grain" leather sofas advertised at $900 and on the next page see "Top- Grain" leather sofas advertised at $2900. Remember, there are no furniture police. You are on your own and if you are not prepared, watch out.

chapter 4

Shopping for Wood Furniture

buying wood furniture on the Internet is certainly fraught with fewer pitfalls than buying upholstered furniture, but you still must be particularly careful about the terminology used in product descriptions. Read carefully, and when you don't understand what you are reading, ask for clarification. All aspects of a well-done wood item will be hidden from you when you are shopping the Internet for furniture. This means that you need to ask good questions of the personnel manning the web site. It is important to keep in mind that all furniture manufacturers, be they high-end (expensive) or low-end (inexpensive), use the same terms when describing their products. It is also important to keep in mind that all wood furniture pieces have the same fundamental parts: All dressers have a top, side panels, drawers, drawer glides, legs (front and back), hardware, a finish, and a back panel. The dresser that will cost $3000 shares these fundamentals with a dresser that will cost $300. The difference is in the details, but the details are hard to discern on a computer screen. The importance of recognized brand names is that these brand names, if you know them and know what they represent, will give you an indication of what quality level to expect. Just like the expectation you get when someone says Mercedes. Here is a checklist of questions to consider when you are trying to decide on wood furniture purchases.

Chapter 4 Shopping for Wood Furniture

The obvious first consideration with wood furniture is the wood used. Does it really make a difference what wood is used? Yes and no. The type of wood (see the wood glossary) is less important than the quality of the wood used and the way it is handled. An item made of cherry is no better or worse than the same item made of walnut or oak based on the fact of the wood species alone. There is good cherry stock and there is bad cherry stock. If the wood has not been properly prepared through air-drying and kiln-drying to the right moisture levels, it will not make a quality piece of furniture.

Take time to study the item you are considering. Even on a computer screen, you can tell if the piece is well proportioned and balanced. A well-designed item has an integrity that you will feel even if you don't understand the technical aspects of it. If the proportions are right, your mind and eye will recognize it. An item that has excessive design details (a Spanish dresser with spurs as hardware would be a good example of this) may be covering up poor design.

Ask how the item is constructed. How are the joints constructed? Are they tongue-and-groove, double-doweled, mortise-and-tenon? Does the piece have "dust bottoms"? Are they made out of wood or cardboard? What kind of drawer glide mechanisms does the item have: metal or wood? Is the back panel inset into the case or is it simply stapled on? Are the drawers dovetailed? All of these questions will equip you with important information.

But wait a minute. Do you think these kinds of questions will actually result in answers you can trust? If you are beginning to think that shopping for furniture on the Internet will be impossible, you have taken an important step in making sure you will use the Internet furniture retailer properly. Obviously, you should only do business with an Internet furniture retailer who can answer your questions and guarantee you will get exactly what you ordered. Steer clear of the retailer who can't answer your questions completely. This is particularly important if you haven't seen the product and can't go somewhere to see it. Finally, if you don't have a 30-day full-refund return privilege, perhaps you should take your business somewhere else. Don't risk buying a "pig in a poke." There are too many places for you to shop to take a chance on any that seem scurrilous.

> Always keep in mind that the difference between an inexpensive item and a quality item consists of more than one thing. Instead of looking for a single $500 difference, look instead for ten $50 differences in a number of different spots. Quality is always a matter of many things done well that collectively add up to a significant price difference.

> Don't be confused by the terms "cherry finish," or "mahogany finish," or "walnut finish," or any wood finish for that matter. Any finish with any name can be put on any wood. A web site or advertisement will often tout a wonderful piece of furniture in a "rich cherry finish" for only $399. Read carefully to see what wood was actually used in the manufacture of the item, and then decide accordingly if the value is there. You might be looking at a "rich cherry finish" on birch. Is that bad? Not necessarily, but don't pay cherry prices for birch pieces.

Does it Matter if Wood Furniture is Solid or Veneered?

Amazingly, in the year 2000, this is still one of the most asked questions I get as I travel around the country. I think it continues to be of concern simply because of the terms used: "solid" sounds so solid, and logic says it must be good if it is solid. Well, the truth is that there are both good and bad examples of solid-wood construction and good and bad examples of veneered construction. The terms "solid" and "veneer" in and of themselves tell you nothing about the quality of the furniture. Trust me: It doesn't matter in a quality or value context.

Let me cite some examples of the dilemma you face when you start trying to build a case for solid over veneer or vice versa. Veneering is a technique that was first developed by the Egyptians over 3000 years ago. Many of the most costly fine antiques that sell for millions of dollars are veneered. Much of the finest furniture produced in the 17th and 18th centuries was veneered. Veneer is the only way the magnificent beauty of a log can be revealed. By contrast, solid-wood techniques were used by country craftsmen not because it was superior construction, but because they lacked the tools and skills (and the customers) to produce veneered furniture. There is nothing inherently special about solid-wood furniture, so stop worrying about it and concern yourself with the real question: Are you getting a quality piece of furniture and is it a value?

Glossary of Woods

A word of caution: Do not put too much importance on the type of wood being used in the furniture you are considering. More important than the type of wood used is how the wood was prepared for manufacturing and whether or not it was a quality piece of wood to begin with. Just because the wood is oak, cherry, or mahogany doesn't tell you anything about how good the wood is. Bottom line: There is a great deal of poor oak, poor cherry, poor mahogany, and poor whatever used to build furniture. Use your head and check it out.

Acacia: A light brown hardwood from Australia and Africa (also down the street from me where it drives all the allergy sufferers crazy when in bloom). In ancient times, acacia was used by Eastern nations for religious and sacred buildings, and is still used in churches and special architectural applications.

Amaranth: This is a South American import with a dark purple-hued color and a very fine-grained texture with good figuring. It is often used in contemporary furniture.

Amboyna: A rich brown, highly figured wood with yellow and red streaks, that is often used for modern furniture. An East Indian wood.

Ash: A hard, dense wood, generally blond to light brown in color, with a good grain resembling oak. This is a very good wood for exposed parts that require strength and a casual appearance.

Bamboo: A woody plant found in tropical forests, generally used for casual furniture. Utilizes leather wraps as fastening devices.

Birch: A very hard fine-grained wood, usually light brown in color, which takes all finishes well, making it the wood of choice when imitating more expensive woods such as mahogany.

Black walnut: A beautiful native wood. Over-cutting in the late 1800s has reduced the supply and driven the price to high levels so it is not used to a great extent today. It is considered by many to be perhaps our most beautiful domestic furniture wood. You will often run into black walnut when you are looking at antiques.

Did you know that today's technology makes it possible for any wood grain to be simulated by a manufacturer and then "printed" on any surface? While this is good for our diminishing forests, it does not make for "fine furniture." Anytime you see a retail price that is too good to be true, make sure you know what you are buying. Remember: While it is true that a manufacturer must state what woods were used in a piece, there is no obligation on the part of the retailer to tell you anything that you don't ask about.

> Phenol and urea, synthetic resins developed in 1940 primarily for use in the aircraft and marine construction industries, have given the furniture industry the perfect adhesive for securing veneer to its core material. The furniture industry had historically relied on animal glues as the chief adhesive used in constructing veneer panels, but these glues were prone to failure due to dampness and changing atmospheric conditions. Synthetic resins are resistant to fungus, heat, cold, salt water, acids—you name it. Veneer panels don't fail anymore, it is that simple.

Butternut: Sometimes called white walnut, since it resembles walnut in all characteristics except color. It is hard, durable, nicely figured, and the trees are found in all parts of the U.S. Butternut has long been favored for carving, but for all of its good qualities it is seldom used today by commercial manufacturers.

Cedar: We all know cedar is very fragrant and has an ancient history of use in furniture. Today its main use is for small chests and drawer liners (as well as specialty boxes for cigars or pencils).

Cherry: One of the "big four furniture woods" along with oak, mahogany, and maple. Cherry is a durable hardwood, reddish-brown in color. It is generally available only from smaller trees, which makes it a challenge for the industry to produce at adequate levels and reasonable prices to meet consumer demand.

Circassian walnut: This is possibly the most handsome of the walnuts. It is a very expensive dark brown wood with a very curly grain that is native to the area around the Black Sea.

Cocobolo: A dark brown wood with a purple cast that is used, for the most part, in the production of contemporary furniture.

Elm: A creamy beige wood with very little contrast in grain or color. It is hard and dense, yet flexible. It is used in the construction of upholstery frames more often than in the construction of wood furniture.

Ebony: This is the dark heartwood from an African tree. Its principal use today is for inlay in fine furniture. With the exception of the most expensive furniture today, this "line effect" is most often silk-screened (or painted), which results in a look that's similar to ebony inlay but at greatly reduced cost.

French burl: This term is often used to describe walnut from Iran. It has a wonderfully swirly, curly grain that makes it difficult to use for veneer, due to the tendency of the wood to separate into its concentric patterns. This, incidentally, is a problem with any burl material and is one reason why burl items can be expensive.

Grafted walnut burl: This burl is located in the graft area where American walnut stock is grafted onto English walnut root stock. After the trees have stopped producing walnuts, the old wood is cut into veneer. This material is very lovely and inexpensive when compared to European walnut veneers.

Kingwood: An import from Brazil and Sumatra, this is a dark brown wood with black and golden-yellow streaks. It is generally used as an accent wood in fine furniture production.

Mahogany: This has long been a favorite of designers, craftsmen, manufacturers, and consumers. It is one of the "big four furniture woods," and well deserves its reputation as perhaps the finest wood for producing furniture. Mahogany has a beautiful reddish color with magnificent grain patterns depending on how it is cut. Mahogany is stable, takes finishes well, and can be polished to a high sheen. It is generally imported from South America and Africa. Keep in mind that there is only one true mahogany (*Swietenia macrophylla*), which is commonly called Honduras mahogany. The other two types, *Khaya ivorensis*, or African mahogany, and *Shorea negrosensis*, or Philippine mahogany, are not true mahoganies and furniture that is produced using these woods should be considerably less expensive than those done in true Honduras mahogany. When you are price-comparing mahogany, be sure you are comparing similar mahogany types. If the furniture salesperson or consultant you are dealing with doesn't know what species of mahogany is being used take your business elsewhere. Every manufacturer states exactly the types of woods used in their products and if someone doesn't know, he or she is either lying or stupid.

Maple: Blond in color, maple is hard and straight-grained generally, but it is also available in curly and bird's-eye variety. A major, if not the major, wood used in the production of Early American-style furniture, maple is also widely used in contemporary designs. Curly and bird's-eye varieties produce beautiful veneer patterns highly favored by designers and consumers.

Myrtle: A beautiful blond wood used most often as an accent wood in fine wood items.

Face veneer used by American manufacturers is generally 1/26 inches to 1/36 inches thick. European manufacturers generally use face veneer that is 1/48 inches thick to 1/50 inches thick. Japanese manufacturers generally use face veneer that is 1/85 inches thick to 1/100 inches thick. Craftsmen who build custom wood furniture and cut their own veneers generally use face veneer that is 1/40 to 1/28 inches thick.

There is only one true furniture mahogany: Honduras mahogany (Swietenia macrophylla). Other types of mahogany can be very attractive, but don't pay Honduras mahogany prices for its honest but poor cousins!

> Are we cutting down the rain forests at such an extent that we are running out of mahogany? The answer depends on who you're talking to. I think everyone would agree, though, that our supply of fine Honduras mahogany is diminishing at too rapid a rate to be casual about it. Cuban Mahogany, which was a magnificent wood, was widely used until the beginning of the 20th century, and is now in extremely limited supply.

> Did you know that mahogany doesn't appeal to wood-eating insects? This is another reason why it was so widely used during the 17th and 18th centuries.

Oak: Possibly the most important wood used in the production of wood furniture from the earliest of times. While there are more than fifty varieties of oak, they all have a similar look, and all are hard and durable. English and French oaks are considered superior to the American variety because of the beauty of their grain patterns.

Olive: A light yellow wood most often used as an accent.

Palisander: A brown wood with a violet cast. This is an import from Brazil and the East Indies, and finds its widest use in modern-style furniture.

Pine: Was one of the major woods for the production of furniture in Early America. It was cheap, easy to work with, easy to paint, and readily available. It was, along with oak, Everyman's furniture wood. There are many varieties of pine and it is a legitimate wood for the production of furniture. Pine is in fact experiencing an important revival today, as it fits neatly into today's' more casual lifestyles. However, unless it is wonderfully painted and in limited editions by a significant manufacturer or craftsman, you should never have to pay too much for a pine furniture piece.

Pecan: A light to reddish brown wood with a pleasing grain pattern. It is a durable, tough wood that was widely used in structural situations in furnituremaking. During the 60s and 70s, it was also used to great effect as a face veneer.

Primavera: Sometimes known as white mahogany, this wood is most often used in drawer bottoms and other inconspicuous furniture parts. You may find it used as a face veneer in less expensive items.

Redwood: Seldom used in furniture items with the exception of outdoor pieces. It is a handsome wood with a uniform red color, and is resistant to insects and water damage. (It is still a good idea to cover or otherwise protect outdoor redwood furniture when it is storming). Redwood, while reddish when new, turns gray as it weathers. Actually, it gets better looking when it weathers.

Rosewood: One of the great decorative woods used in the production of fine furniture. It is reddish-brown in color with black streaks. The Brazilian variety, called jacaranda, is considered the finest variety.

Satinwood: A light blond wood with a satiny finish and wonderful grain pattern. It is a very expensive import from India that is chiefly used as an accent wood in only the very finest furniture.

Teak: This wood can range in color from yellow to brown. It is even more durable than oak. It has principally been used in shipbuilding but can also be found today in outdoor furnishings. You may even run across it being used for contemporary furniture. When used in fine outdoor furniture, teak is rarely finished, to allow it to weather to a pretty gray patina.

Walnut: This wood is not widely used by present-day manufacturers, but it has been in different eras one of the premier woods for the finest furniture. A beautiful light brown with gray overtones, walnut is found in the forests of North America, Europe, and Africa. It is, of course, a major commercial nut tree, and while extensively planted for its nut production, walnut is not readily available as a furniture wood.

Yew: This is a close-grained hardwood that is deep red-brown in color. The tree is an evergreen that thrives in England and has a grain pattern that is similar to bird's-eye maple. Since it is so much more costly than maple, the wood is generally used only as an accent wood.

Zebrawood: A golden-yellow wood with dark brown stripes. It is most often used as an accent wood.

> The natural color of any wood is generally of little concern to today's manufacturers, since they can color any wood any way they want. A wood is selected by a manufacturer based more on its grain characteristics, cost, and availability. Often the natural color of a wood will be bleached out prior to the selected finish color being applied.

> Keep in mind that any "casual styled" item can be a license for the manufacturer to cut corners. This can certainly be okay, but the price you pay should reflect the more "casual concerns" that went into production.

chapter 5

*U*nderstanding the Retailer

Today almost all manufacturers and major retailers, with all of the collective brands involved, are on the Internet. Everyone is rushing to have a web site. In fact, if you put www. in front of almost any brand and then put a .com (www.almostanything.com) at the end, you will probably pull up a web site telling you all about it. But you will not be able to order merchandise on most of these web sites. Most major furniture manufacturers have been, and are, restricting the sale of their merchandise to their local stores and outlets. They are not allowing the sale of their product from any web site. Why? The simple answer is that they do not want to hurt the retail sales of their local dealers. Is this fair? Is this pro-consumer? Don't you end up paying more money than you need to by having to buy from a local merchant? Not necessarily. In fact, overall this is the big question that faces the Internet shopper: Is buying on the Internet a "better deal" than buying from the local merchant? Only you can answer this question because there are so many variables in buying furniture.

To give a simple insight into the process: I buy a lot of books. I know I can often pay less by ordering a book from an Internet retailer, but I also know that I love to go into bookstores. The dollar I save on the Internet just isn't any fun for me. I need to go to the store. Since furniture shopping is so much more complicated than book shopping, and the dollars involved are so much more significant, this may not be a fair comparison, but it is important to keep in mind how and what you like to experience when you shop for anything anywhere.

Chapter 5 Understanding the Retailer

How its products are presented to the public is a legitimate concern of any manufacturer. If a manufacturer does not require proper display and customer service, ultimately consumers will be the loser. But like any paternalistic approach to control, for the sake of all concerned, a moment comes when the concern and requirements begin to outweigh the benefits that are intended. Frankly, this is the current state of affairs in the furniture industry. It is no secret that consumers could get better prices by buying from the North Carolina outlets. If you want to see furniture dealers turn red with frustration and fury, mention that you are considering buying furniture from a North Carolina outlet. Incidentally, don't do this to any dealer who looks unhealthy to begin with or you may end up having to give CPR. Mention to most furniture manufacturers that it seems strange that they are so sanctimonious about restricting the sale of their products on the Internet when they actively sell their products to North Carolina Furniture outlets and watch it shipped all over the U.S. Are we missing something? Sure we are. What we are missing is an equal opportunity to share in better prices.

In all fairness, it must be stated that what we have in a furniture store is a local opportunity to see merchandise nicely displayed and ready for delivery to our homes. This local opportunity is the result of a company risking a great deal of money to provide you with a local showcase. This is no small thing, and I have said repeatedly that when shopping for furniture it is important to see the merchandise before you buy it. So what is right? To compound the problem, we now have the Internet store bringing all sorts of product into your home. Will the complications never cease?

Try to remember that these are good complications for consumers, because what they mean is that local retailers and manufacturers, along with the new Internet furniture retailers and the greatly improved North Carolina furniture outlets, will have to come up with a game plan that benefits everyone. They will do this because you the consumer have the ultimate vote and will determine just what you want. By the way you spend your dollars, the rest of the players in the game will make the necessary adjustments or end up out of the game.

Coping with Information Overload

How do you handle all this information and how do you best use it? It will be important to keep in mind how the World Wide Web is organizing itself. Some of the top fifteen Internet furniture stores that I have listed represent what is called a major portal, or "megasite," which means that these sites feature a multitude of manufacturers all showing their wares on the site with specific links to each of their home sites. The megasites are GoodHome.com, Furniture.com, and Living.com, etc. Specific sites like EddieBauer.com, J.C.Penney.com, and Macys.com are all specific to their own programs, and while they probably will offer links to major suppliers, they will not represent as broad a lineup of product as a megasite. So if you are at the beginning of your shopping experience, it is probably best to start with the megasites and get more specific as you narrow down your search. It isn't a whole lot different from getting into your car and starting to drive around town. I would expect you would go to the big stores first to see what they have and then start looking at the smaller specialists. Remember the World Wide Web is a marketplace just like a large city in many respects. The big difference is that instead of taking cars, cabs, subways, and busses to get around, you and your mouse are doing the walking.

A major concern of all Internet merchants is how to get people to visit their web sites. Today's consumer does not have the time or desire to drive all over town looking for a product. Today's consumer wants to go to a spot, see everything quickly, then compare one product to another. The same is true for the World Wide Web. In the furniture world, companies such as Ethan Allen, Thomasville, Drexel-Heritage, and La-Z-Boy all have enough stature to stand on their own, but even they realize the value of being exposed on megasites. As a comparison, just think of how, not too long ago, automobile dealerships were scattered all over town. The thought was that an exclusive site gave each manufacturer an advantage. Then it began to dawn on the dealers that perhaps it would be better to be near one another in the hopes that proximity would increase traffic. We then got "auto rows," and now, in most major metro areas, it is not uncommon to see car dealers grouped side by side in mega auto malls.

My Shopping Suggestion

Visit the megasites! Go to HomePortfolio.com, Living.com, Furniture.com, GoodHome.com, or HomePoint.com, and wander through the site looking for the styles and considerations that are important to you. As you narrow your search into specific design and price areas, link to the referred sites in an effort to expand your understanding of that category or manufacturer. Often when you link to participating merchants or manufacturers, they in turn will link you to other related sites.

Visit the web site of a particular manufacturer if it hasn't turned up as a link on one of the megasites. What do you do if you can't figure out the address or you can't quite remember the name? Go to www.furnituretoday.com, which is the web site of *Furniture Today*, the trade magazine of the furniture industry. They have on their web site a comprehensive list of almost all of the manufacturers and related home furnishing businesses, and in most cases they will have a direct link to the business you're interested in. You can also go to my web site, www.furnitureideas.com, and request information about any manufacturer and I will get back to you via email with the information you need.

When you feel you are nearing a decision on a product and have been quoted a price, get a price quote on the same product from one of the North Carolina factory outlet sites. Remember, anytime you are comparing the prices of one site or merchant with another, make sure the price quote includes (or doesn't include) the following: shipping costs, set-up costs, and insurance (if needed). If you do not compare items that are exactly the same in all aspects, you will not be able to tell which deal is best. Don't forget to check with your local dealer to see if that "deal" is as good or better. Good shopping is the result of careful and thoughtful research. Not only do you end up with the best possible results, you learn a lot along the way.

It is important to realize that shopping the Internet for furniture is not going to be a snap. For all of the Internet's highly touted speed, you will end up spending considerable time watching pictures download on your screen, clicking from one site to another, downloading information, waiting for email replies, chasing style categories, trying to "read" small picture details, and so on. But you will inevitably realize that the Internet is a highly efficient tool that allows you to view an incredible array of furniture—at your own convenience. In addition, once you get on the Internet and into the megasites, they will start emailing you interesting information (if you give them your email address) about the furniture world. For instance, while working on this book, I once checked my email before beginning a writing session in my word-processing program. There was mail from Living.com telling me that I had just received their March newsletter. I clicked on and the newsletter was marvelous—colorful, fact-filled, and very interesting. Just what information did the newsletter bring to me? First of all, there was a terrific article on the "Anatomy of a Sofa." It was so good that I wish I had written it myself! In response to consumer's inquiries, there was a selection of interesting answers, with pictures of design and decorating tips. I did click on the page of "baker's racks," and saw pictures of sixteen racks from $349 to $1,829. Several pictures did not have a price quoted and it was stated that the manufacturer did not allow the prices to be printed but that they could be emailed to me. I asked for two prices. There was also a wonderful article on fabrics. I could go on, but I think you get the picture. Was it trouble-free? In one respect the newsletter did illustrate a point you have to keep in mind when shopping on the Internet. The article I loved on sofas was wonderfully informative, but did the information apply to every sofa offered on the site? I think not.

Information is power, as I have often said, but information that is stored and not used is no better than a locked library. Remember, don't be seduced by the information and then assume that all the elements of the program fit the ideal. Be sharp. But with that proviso, think back on the number of times you have gone into your local stores and tried to get information on anything. Did you ever come back from a local furniture store trip and feel that you had really learned something? I'll bet not often. Information is the great gift the Internet brings to us. In fact, you will end up better informed than most floor sales personnel—a sad commentary. Hopefully, the smart ones will be shopping the Internet, too.

Let's get specific and see how Gomez.com ranks the furniture web sites they track on a regular basis. Gomez.com is the self-styled "eCommerce Authority." It is important while reviewing the rankings to keep in mind that all Internet furniture retailers are relatively new businesses.

These retailers may not be new to furniture retailing, but they are new to Internet retailing—and constantly experimenting with how best to present themselves to the consumer. I mention this because Gomez.com can be brutal in its comments on the performance of the sites. This level of honesty is what you need, though. It doesn't do any good if a rating service has nothing but nice things to say about everything. It just isn't so in the real world. The best retailers—Bloomingdale's, Neiman Marcus, Tiffany's—all can deliver below-par service to someone at some point in time. No system is perfect. What you want to see is consistent performance at the highest levels over a significant period of time. Right now we don't have any long-term consistency to key on, but several current Internet furniture retailers are doing an excellent job and many of the rest are working hard to improve their presentations. I mention this not because I think you should be forgiving in your personal evaluation of any site, but rather because I hope you will continually update your personal ratings of a site and not give it just one chance at this early stage of the game.

One final thought to keep in mind: I think the Gomez.com ratings are extremely valuable, but remember that they do not rate or comment on the furniture that any of the Internet sites feature. Frankly, to expect them to do so would be expecting too much, since Gomez.com personnel are not furniture experts. But since one of your biggest concerns is what furniture to buy, you must remember that you can't assume a highly rated site will carry highly rated furniture. The one doesn't necessarily follow the other, and that is why I have spent so much time talking to you about furniture per se. When in doubt, look to Gomez.com for points concerning customer service, customer feedback, graphic display, shipping concerns, consumer comments, etc. (In fact, you should bookmark Gomez.com and check it when shopping for anything—it's that valuable a reference.) But when it comes to buying Brand X or Brand Z, call or email me, check with an interior design consultant, or visit a local furniture retailer.

Internet Furniture Sites Ranked by Gomez.com

1. GoodHome.com
    www.goodhome.com

2. Furniture.com
    www.furniture.com

3. Living.com
    www.living.com

4. FurnitureFind.com
    www.furniturefind.com

5. HomePoint.com
    www.homepoint.com

6. EddieBauer
    www.eddiebauer.com

7. BeHome
    www.behome.com

8. RTA Online
    www.rtaonline.com

9. Bombay Company
    www.bombay.com

10. Puerta Bella
    www.puertabella.com

11. FurnitureOnline.com
    www.furnitureonline.com

12. J.C. Penney
    www.jcpenney.com

13. EZshop.com
    www.ezshop.com

14. Postvictorian.com
    www.postvictorian.com

15. Home 123
    www.home123furniture.com

16. AffordableFurniture.com
    www.affordablefurniture.com

17. Furniture Plaza
    www.furnitureplaza.com

Notice that GoodHome.com edged out Furniture.com in the Gomez.com ratings shown. Does this mean that GoodHome.com had the best lineup of furniture for sale? Not at all. It simply means that the site personnel did the best job with what they had and a majority of consumers who used their facility were satisfied. I am not splitting hairs. Obviously, in the absence of any other data, a high rating by Gomez.com is certainly a good indication that you should take a serious look at GoodHome.com as a site to find the furniture you want. What I am trying to do is to liberate you from the hype, advertising, sales pitches, and allure of third-party experts and make you your own expert You will then know what to look for so that you can make solid judgments that will give you more value and bring you more satisfaction in your furniture shopping. After saying this, let's take a look at each site and see what it's all about.

Before we get down to specifics, it's important to look at how Gomez.com arrives at its ratings. They rate each site for ease of use, customer confidence, on-site resources, and relationship services. They then further refine the evaluation by considering the experience level of the shopper: Consumers are grouped into the categories of enthusiast, first-time buyer, and one-stop buyer. This gives a solid look at the Internet store and the kind of people who have used the store's services. Gomez.com even offers an on-line collection of consumer reviews of each store. You will see comments ranging from the "best experience ever" to "I would never shop there again." This kind of range, from wonderful to dismal, is to be expected and should not deter you from shopping at highly rated sites if the preponderance of reviews is good. Let's face it, you cannot satisfy everyone no matter what you do. But complaints are a clue, and if you see yourself in someone else's feedback, pay attention and think about how you handle things. For instance, if you are a stickler for detail and time frames, it will be critical to question site personnel closely on these matters.

I am not going to go into a great deal of detail on the hows, whys, and whos of the Gomez.com ratings, because the ratings could change over time. The "best" could easily slip down the ratings slide, and an "also ran" could scale the ladder. It is certainly the nature of businesses to strive to improve but, unfortunately, it is also the nature of businesses to rest on their laurels. This is going to be particularly true of Internet businesses, where the speed of change is like nothing we have ever encountered before. Whenever you are on the Internet shopping, go to Gomez.com for the latest rankings and evaluation of the Internet stores you are looking at. Then go to Furnitureideas.com for my take on the actual furniture items you are considering. This combination of Gomez.com and Furnitureideas.com is an unbeatable source of consumer research and furniture expertise that will give you the best independent information on smart furniture shopping available today.

1. www.goodhome.com: Rated #1 by Gomez.com and highly praised in all categories with the exception of its on-line resources (design information, on-line chat function), GoodHome.com was highest rated for first-time buyers. This company offers a money-back return policy, which is very important (you always need to know who pays the freight both ways on problems). Absolutely a must-visit Internet furniture retail site.

2. www.furniture.com: Rated #2 by Gomez.com, but very close in its numerical average to GoodHome.com. A very significant print media advertiser, you have probably seen Furniture.com ads on TV and in the papers. Given the very highest praise for its online tools and designer assistance, this is a must-visit Internet furniture retail site. The only negative feedback was that the tested consumer feedback was lacking. This can happen to the best of businesses on a random basis, but it should always be a concern for management. Very important for you is a recently announced 30-day money back guarantee. Return shipping is covered as well. The company apparently had a "satisfaction guaranteed" policy, but changed it to the above. Thirty days with freight paid is solid enough. Don't miss this site!

3. www.living.com: Rated #3 by Gomez.com but still very close numerically to #1 and #2. Absolutely a superior furniture Internet retailer. This company has a "partnership" with Amazon.com, which could potentially be very productive and could send what is already an excellent company to unknown heights. Keep an eye on this one and, certainly, when you are doing your online furniture shopping, this is a must-visit site. Rated #1 for the "enthusiast" and "one-stop shopper," and given high praise for its interactive room-designer tool and layout, it is almost trouble-free to navigate. The only negative note was that all items were not priced and that you had to email for those prices. I checked that out and received an email response within the day with a price and link to the supplier of the item. I think the company handled the situation very well.

4. www.furniturefind.com: Rated #4 by Gomez.com but #1 in "customer confidence," this is one of the older Internet furniture retailers. FurnitureFind.com has one of the largest assortments of home furnishings on the Internet. This should be one of your must-visit sites when shopping. FurnitureFind.com was recently purchased by GoodHome.com, a combination likely to be good for consumers. The only negative about furniturefind.com is an antiquated site design and a lack of interactive tools. The new combination of GoodHome.com and FurnitureFind.com should fix that up nicely. According to Gomez.com, GoodHome.com and FurnitureFind.com will run parallel for a time, and then FurnitureFind.com will be blended into the GoodHome.com program. A very, very good Internet furniture retailer just got better.

5. www.homepoint.com: Rated #5, this site is highly praised for its content and decorating ideas. A very good site with one glaring negative cited—the company's reluctance or inability to mail out fabric swatches. If this policy is firm, I would not buy upholstered items from this company. It is that simple. The site is well worth checking out because its overall rating is good, but make sure you check all the details.

6. www.eddiebauer.com: Inexplicably rated #6 by Gomez.com as an Internet furniture retailer, Eddie Bauer is a wonderful company, but the amount of furniture this company handles simply doesn't merit the #6 slot. Absolutely go to Eddie Bauer for many things, but if you are looking for variety and options in furniture, go to other sites first.

7. www.behome.com: Rated #7 and praised for its content, it was noted that the site structure was getting in the way of easy navigation. If this is a site's biggest problem, we could all live with structural problems, but BeHome.com apparently has other issues in that it charges a 10 percent restocking fee and there is no "satisfaction guaranteed" policy. This is too competitive an arena to play craps with your furniture purchases. No guarantee and restocking fees? Watch out!

8. www.rtaonline.com: Rated #8, but has little to recommend it unless you are looking for ready-to-assemble furniture. While much can be said for RTA furniture as a category, this is not a site to shop unless you are specifically looking for RTA product.

9. www.bombay.com is rated #9, but with restocking fees of 20 percent and little content, you will be better off going to their physical stores. I like Bombay, but I am not impressed with their Internet efforts.

10. www.puertabella.com This company is rated #10, and while this may not be particularly impressive, this is a new company that is very much into offering decorating assistance. Gomez.com feels it is a real comer and deserves a look. My recommendation is to take a look but be careful.

The Internet furniture retailers rated 11 through 17 all offer a minimum of reasons to recommend them compared to the top five sites. My suggestion is that you concentrate on the top five and check back on any site that needs to upgrade its efforts.

Chapter 5 Understanding the Retailer

My Personal Favorite Internet Furniture Web Sites (for both new and antique furniture)

- DK Antiques, Ltd. www.dkantiques.com
  (wonderful selection in New York City)
- M.S. Rau Antiques: www.rauantiques.com
  (an always stunning selection in New Orleans)
- Habite: www.habite.com
  (magnificent French furnishings in San Francisco)
- Valerio: www.valerioartdeco.com
  (wonderful selection of Art Deco in Miami)
- Bernhardt: www.bernhardtfurniture.com
  (one of our best manufacturers of wood furniture)
- Guy Chaddock & Co: www.guychaddock.com
  (magnificent wood furniture, my personal favorite)
- Kreiss: www.kreiss.com
  ("contemporized" traditional master works in wood)
- Roche Bobois: www.roche-bobois.com
  (always exciting creations in wood and upholstery)
- Century Furniture: www.centuryfurniture.com
  (always does a wonderful job of combining style, execution, and price)
- Statesville Chair Company: www.statesvillechair.com
  (wonderful upholstery with a great deal of style)
- Patina: www.patinainc.com ("to the trade only," which means you will have to get your designer to obtain it for you, but if you are looking for outstanding painted wood furniture you will find it here. Expensive but worth it.)
- McGuire: www.mcguirefurniture.com
  (the best in rattan; style and execution—they have it all)
- AmericanLeather: www.americanleather.com
  (one of our best leather producers—wonderful style, flawless execution, and top quality)
- Fremarc Designs: www.fremarc.com
  (absolutely beautiful furniture)
- Emerson Et Cie: www.emersonetcie.com (some of the best values and most exciting occasional and accent items from any source. You must spend some time looking over this site. You won't be sorry you did.)
- Burton-Ching: www.burtonching.com (I just spent some time in their San Francisco Showroom and the furniture is magnificent—expensive but worth every penny)
- Great Gatsby's Antiques: www.greatgatsbys.com
  (a great deal of "over the top" furniture is featured in their catalog, but on the other hand you can make some important statements at surprisingly good prices)

The Very Latest Entries Into the Internet Furniture Field that May Prove To Be the Prototype for the Future

Ultimately, I believe that consumers will have the advantage of the best of all worlds in furniture shopping, with Internet sites that provide state-of-the-art graphics, in-depth information services on product, product and price comparison information, and interior design assistance. A local network of stores and designers will back up all of this so that consumers will be able to confirm and support their home-furnishing decisions by seeing the product and talking to home-furnishings professionals.

www.homeportfolio.com: This is the type of home furnishings web site that may well be the best of all worlds for the consumer. Tom Ashbrook, the co-founder, is quoted as saying about his web business: "It is not an online store but rather a portfolio site organized around consumers' interests and experience." Ashbrook goes on to say, "We're looking to drive traffic into stores, not out of them." This is exactly what I think the consumer needs. Furniture shopping can be such a wonderful experience that the thought of it simply being a web adventure leaves me cold. I think Ashbrook is right on target. They have assembled an impressive group of manufacturers who are participants in the HomePortfolio program: Baker, Century, Hickory Chair, Lexington, McGuire, Mitchell Gold, and Swaim. homeportfolio.com is concentrating on the premium players in home furnishings. You should take a look and see what they are up to.

www.homepoint.com: This is another effort to bring together all the elements in home furnishings into a package that plays to the strengths of each element. It is becoming more and more recognized that a local dealer is key to making any on-line effort successful over the long term.

www.buymart.com: This is an informational web service for casual furniture. According to the owner, Rudy Davis, this site is more of a referral service than an e-retailing site. Actually, this is what you need more than an on-line ordering opportunity. You need information, and then you need to know where you can go to see the product. Just think how much more powerful your shopping efforts will be when you can go into a local store knowing exactly how its product relates to competing product. You can then decide what product is best for you.

Internet Furniture Retailers and/or Manufacturers Where You Can Order On Line

- A C Furniture: www.acfurniture.com
- Agrell and Thorpe: www.agrellandthorpe.com
- Amish Furniture: www.amish1.com
- Amish Furniture: www.amishfurniture.com
- Bar Stools: www.barstoolemporium.com
- Bar Stools: www.barstools-to-go.com
- Barn Furniture Mart: www.barnfurnituremart.com
- Blackwelders Catalog: www.blackwelder.com (a North Carolina player well worth a look)
- Bombay Company: www.bombayco.com (excellent, affordable, take a look)
- Bookouts: www.bookouts.com (well worth a look)
- Bubble Furniture: www.bubblefurniture.com (with this name you have to look)
- Butcher Block Barn: www.butcherblockbarn.com
- Champagne: www.champagnefurniture.com
- Concordian Chesterfield: www.concordian.com
- Cyberwood Express: www.woodexpress.com
- Décor Direct: www.decordirect.com
- Discount Beds: www.discountbeds.com
- Don Andres Designers: www.donandres.com
- Dopko Furniture Co: www.dopko.com
- Equator Imports: www.equatorimp.com
- Everything Amish: www.everythingamish.com (if you like country)
- Falls Leather: www.fallsleather.com
- Foam Mart: www.foammart.com
- Furniture Direct: www.furnituredir.com
- Furniture Direct: www.furnituredirect.com
- Furniture DotCom: www.furniture.com
- Furniture Find: www.furniturefind.com (worth a look)
- Furniture In The Raw West: www.iircreate.com
- Furniture Network: www.kfnet.com
- Fusion Coatings: www.fusioncoatings.com

Shopping for Furniture on the Internet

Internet Furniture Retailers and/or Manufacturers Where You Can Order On Line (cont.)

- Gran America: www.granamerica.com
- Hickory Chair: www.hickorychair.com
  (always worth a look)
- Crafthome.com: www.craft-home.com
  (an arts and craft site)
- Design Concepts Unlimited: www.dcuinc.com
- Formdecor.com: www.formdecor.com
  (a "vintage" furniture site)
- Furniture On The Internet: www.furnitureontheInternet.com
- George Smith.com: www.georgesmith.com
  (features handmade English seating)
- HomePoint.com: www.homepoint.com
  (a "megasite" to carefully check)
- Industrial House: www.industrialhouse.com
- Iron Table: www.irontable.com
- KDS Designs: www.kdsdesigns.com
- Kozyhome.Com: www.kozyhome.com
  (promises 30-day delivery and 30-day return privileges!)
- Leather Magic: www.leathermagic.com
- Leo Burke Furniture: www.leoburke.com
- Log Furniture: www.logfurniture.com
- Mathis Brothers: www.mathisbrothers.com
  (shouldn't miss this site)

Internet Furniture Retailers and/or Manufacturers Where You Can Order On Line (cont.)

- Mayfield Leather: www.mayfieldseating.com
- Midlothian: www.realteak.com
- Modernhome.com: www.modernhome.com (contemporary style furnishings)
- Museum of Modern Art: www.store.moma.com (definitely for the modernist)
- PAS Classic Steel Co: www.pasclassic.com
- Plunkett Furniture: www.plunkettfurniture.com (excellent stores, Chicago and St. Louis)
- PVC Patio: www.pvcpatio.com
- Refinishing Store: www.refinish.com
- Sofa and Chair: www.sofaandchair.com
- SportASeat.com: www.sportaseat.com
- Sunlite Sales: www.sunlitesales.com
- Times Table: www.timestable.com
- TLC Distributing: www.tlcdistributing.com
- Unicahome.com: www.unicahome.com (modern and contemporary showcase)
- Wickes Furniture: www.wickesfurniture.com (should check them out)
- World2Market.com: www.world2market.com (furniture from rural America, Africa)

Internet Furniture Web Sites for Information Only

In almost all cases, these sites will direct you to local stores to see the merchandise. Frankly, I think this is a wise way to go.

- Adamstand: www.adamstandworkbenches.com
- Aktrin: www.aktrin.com
- American Custom Marble: www.acmarbleinc.com
- American Interiors: www.aminteriors.com
- American Office: www.aofurn.com
- Artifacts Fine Furniture: www.artifactsfurn.com
- August Design: www.augustdesign.com
- Aunt Zelda's: www.auntzelda.com
  (you can't resist a name like this)
- Auton Company: www.auton.com
- Avant-Scene: www.avant-scene.com
- Axxent: www.axxentonline.com
- Ayers Amish Furniture: www.amishhouse.com
  (wonderful country look)
- Badcock Furniture: www.badcock.com
- Barcalounger: www.barcalounger.com
  (you should look if you need a recliner)
- Bassett Furniture: www.bassettfurniture.com
  (great starter furniture)
- Bent Log Designs: www.bentlog.com
- Berkeley Mills: www.berkeley-mills.com
- Berkline: www.berkline.com (should take a look)
- Berne Furniture: www.berne.com
- Bernie and Phyl's: www.bernphyl.com
- Better Living: www.btrlvg.com
- Billy Bags: www.billybags.com (love the name)
- Blue Tomatoes: www.bluetomatoes.com
  (how can you resist going to Blue Tomatoes?)
- Brixey Corp: www.brixey.com

Internet Furniture Web Sites for Information Only (cont.)

- Brown Furniture: www.brownfurniture.com
- Bucks County: www.buckscountyfurn.com
  (if you like country take a look)
- Buck's Unpainted: www.bucksunpaintedfurn.com
- Buddy Rhodes Studio: www.buddyrhodes.com
- Canwood Furniture: www.canwood.com
- Capell's Lawn and Leisure: www.capellco.com
- Chair King: www.chairking.com
- Chameleon Systems: www.smartfurniture.com
- Cherry Hill: www.cherryhillfurn.com
- Ciron: www.central-iron.com.sg
- Classiconline: www.classiconline.com
- Clear Cut Acrylics: www.clearcutacrylics.com
- Coja Leatherline: www.coja.com
- Colby Furniture: www.colbyfurniture.com
- Collection Reproduction: www.colrep.com
- Computer Comforts: www.computercomforts.com
- Concepts For Today: www.conceptsfortoday.com
- Conley Stacking Sys: www.conleystacker.com
- Contemporary: www.contemporarydesign.com
- Creative Seatings: www.have-a-seat.com
- DAMAC: www.damac.com
- Danish Designs: www.danishdesigns.com
- Dazzle Glass: www.dazzleglass.com
- De Boer's Furniture: www.deboers.com
- Desience Corporation: www.desience.com
- Design Centro Italia: www.italydesign.com
- Design Craft: www.designcraft.com
- Domain Home: www.domain-home.com
  (well worth going to)
- Dovetails: www.dovetails.com
  (I would check anything with a name like this)

Internet Furniture Web Sites for Information Only (cont.)

- Drexel Heritage: www.drexelheritage.com (don't miss this site)
- Ecologic: www.ecoloft.com
- Electro-Kinetics: www.electrokinetics.com
- Ergonomic Workstation: www.ergo-ws.com
- Eurodesign: www.eurodsgn.com
- European Importers: www.eurofurniture.com
- Falcon: www.falconproducts.com
- Fauxstone: www.stone1.com
- Fine Art Repro: www.fineartrepro.com
- Fine Furnishings by Seldens: www.seldens.com
- Fleet Plummer: www.fleetplummer.com
- Fletcher Cameron: www.fletchercameron.com
- Flexsteel Industries: www.flexsteel.com (very good upholstery values)
- Flying Turtle Gallery: www.flyingturtle.com (would go for the name alone)
- Four Star Systems: www.fourstarsystems.com
- Frank Chervan: www.chervan.com
- Franklin Corporation: www.franklincorp.com
- Fujian: www.furniturefujian.com
- Furnitureland South: www.furniturelandsouth.com (one of the Big Four in North Carolina)
- Furniture Classics: www.furniture-usa.com
- Furniture Home: www.furniture-home.com
- Furnitureideas.com: www.furnitureideas.com (My site! Best for information!)
- Furniture Maine: www.furnituremaine.com
- Furniture Medic: www.furnituremedic.com
- Furniture Site: www.furnituresite.com
- Garden Room: www.gardenroom.com

Internet Furniture Web Sites for Information Only (cont.)

- Gardiners Furniture: www.gardiners.com
- Golden Technologies: www.goldentech.com
- Grafco: www.grafco.com
- Grolls Fine Furniture: www.grolls.com
- Gruppo Faber: www.fabermobili.com
- Hancock & Moore: www.hancockandmoore.com (wonderful leather furniture)
- Harden Fine Furniture: www.harden.com (outstanding wood furniture)
- Harlee International Futons: www.harlee.com
- Harlem Furniture: www.harlemfurniture.com (well worth a look)
- Harry Art Furniture: www.harryartfurniture.com
- Haverty's: www.havertys.com (very big retail chain, should take a look)
- Heilig Meyers: www.heiligmeyers.com (major retail chain, must take a look)
- Hickory Park: www.hickorypark.com
- Holmes Wilson: www.holmeswilsonfurniture.com
- Home Works: www.homeworksfurniture.com
- House of Bedrooms: www.houseofbedrooms.com
- D&A: www.id-a.com
- Jack Robbins Furniture: www.jackrobbins.com
- Jackson Moore: www.jacksonmoore.com
- Jasper Cabinet: www.jaspercabinetcompany.com (wonderful cabinets)
- Jay Rambo Company: www.jayrambo.com
- Kirklands: www.kirklands.com
- Klaussner/Sealy: www.sealyfurniture.com (should check them out)
- Knox Furniture: www.knoxfurniture.com
- Kohler Co: www.kohlerco.com

Internet Furniture Web Sites for Information Only (cont.)

- Ladd Furniture: www.laddfurniture.com
  (worth a look)
- Laitala Ltd: www.laitala.com
- Lampa: www.lampa.com
- Landscape Forms: www.landscapeforms.com
- Lane Furniture Company: www.lanefurniture.com
  (always worth a look)
- LaStrada: www.lastrada.com
- La-Z-Boy: www.lazboy.com
  (must always look here for upholstery)
- Leather Center: www.leathercenter.com
- Leather Shoppes: www.leathershoppes.com
- Levitz: www.levitz.com (large chain)
- Liberty Metals: www.libertymetals.com
- Lloyd Flanders: www.lloydflanders.com
- Lovelace Interiors: www.lovelace-interiors.com
- Mairal SA: www.mairal.com
- Mallory's Fine Furniture: www.mallorys.com
  (a North Carolina player, always check it out)
- Master Sofa: www.mastersofa.com
- McMinn's Furniture: www.mcminns.com
- Miller Greene: www.millergreene.com
- Mitchell Gold: www.mitchellgold.com
  (well worth a look for upholstery)
- Modern Living: www.modernliving.com
- Montage: www.montageweb.com
- Natuzzi: www.natuzzi.com
  (very affordable leather furniture, major producer)
- Nord Furn: www.nord-furn.com
- Norwalk Furniture: www.norwalkfurniture.com
  (very nice selection)
- O'Sullivan Industries: www.osullivan.com

Internet Furniture Web Sites for Information Only (cont.)

- Pearson Furniture: www.pearsoncompany.com
  (worth a look)
- Pier 1: www.pier1.com
  (always take a look, affordable and interesting)
- Peter Mandel: www.petermandel.com
- Peterson Design: www.petersondesign.com
- Radelow Custom: www.customwooddesigns.com
- Raymour & Flanigan: www.raymourflanigan.com
  (anyone in the Northeast should have a look)
- Rekha Décor: www.rekhadecor.com
- Reupholstering: www.reupholstering.com
  (would check as point of reference)
- Richwell Galleries: www.richwellfurniture.com
- Rio Imports: www.rioimports.com
- Rita's Furniture: www.ritasfurniture.com
- Rizhao Sanmu Corporation: www.sanmu.com
- Roberd's: www.roberdsinc.com
  (worth a look, big company)
- Rohani Furniture: www.rohanifurn.com
- Room Plus: www.roomplus.com (should check them out)
- Rose Furniture: www.rosefurniture.com
  (one of the North Carolina Big Four, a favorite of mine)
- Sabana International: www.sabana.com
- Schwark Furniture: www.schwark.com
- Scottbower Safa Systems: www.scottbower.com
- Seaman Furniture: www.seamans.com
  (always check if you live in the East)
- Shaw Furniture: www.shawfurniture.com
  (check out this North Carolina company)
- Signature Leather: www.signatureleather.com
- Signature Sofa: www.signatureinteriors.com
- Slumberland: www.slumberland-furniture.com

Shopping for Furniture on the Internet

Internet Furniture Web Sites for Information Only   (cont.)

- Sonorma: www.sonorma.com
- Storehouse: www.storehousefurniture.com
- Strouds: www.strouds.com (well worth several looks)
- Strippers: www.the-strippers.com
  (I wouldn't be able to resist)
- Stylus Sofas: www.stylussofas.com
- Techline: www.techlinerockford.com
  (excellent for the money, take a look)
- Teknomet: www.teknomet.com
- Thomasville Furniture: www.thomasville.com
  (a major manufacturer)
- Tig Industries: www.tiginc.com
- Topline Furniture: www.toplinefurniture.com
- Tricolour: www.tricolour.com
- United Teak: www.united-teak.com
- Vesco: www.vesco.com
- Wicker Décor: www.wickdecor.com
- Wood Country: www.woodcountry.com
- Wood Works: www.wood-works.com
- Woodpeckers: www.woodpeckers.com (I couldn't resist)
- Work Spaces: www.workspaces.com
- Workstation Environments: www.workenv.com
- Zagaroli Leather: www.zagorolileather.com
  (very, very nice leather, take a look)

Furniture Web Sites with a Catalog Program and Most Often a Store Program but No Sales On Line

- 101 Furniture: www.101furniture.com
- Hot Site Action Lane: www.action-lane.com
  (always look at a Lane site)
- Adirondack Rustic Designs: www.adkdesign.com
  (if you like unique country, try it)
- Adorable Backyard: www.cedarlawnfurniture.com
- Advance Furniture: www.advancefurniture.com
- Advance Furniture: www.afo.com
- All Wood: www.allwoodfurniture.com
- American Oak: www.americanoak.com
- Amish Wood: www.amishwood.com (fine country looks)
- Anthro Corporation: www.anthro.com
- Antler Art Studio: www.antler-art.com
- Ashley Furniture: www.ashleyfurniture.com
- Avenrich Furniture: www.avenrich.com
- Ballard Designs: www.ballard-designs.com
- BDI: www.bdiusa.com
- Bell'Oggetti: www.belloggetti.com
- Biomorph Desk: www.biomorph-desk.com
- Bolstad Woodworks: www.bolstadwood.com
- Boyles: www.boyles.com
  (one of the North Carolina Big Four, a wonderful source)
- Broadway Furnishings: www.bhfchicago.com
- Canadian Timber: www.canadiantimber.com
- Chairs Int'l: www.chairsint.com
- Cort Furniture: www.cort1.com
- Curran Furniture: www.curran-aat.com
- Danish Design: www.danishdesign-usa.com
- Dansk Furnishings: www.danskfurnishings.com
- Dinettes Plus: www.dinettes.com
- Domestic Temples: www.domestictemple.com
- Dovetail Woodworks: www.dovetailww.com
  (love the name)

Furniture Web Sites with a Catalog Program and Most Often a Store Program but No Sales On Line (cont.)

- Elkhorn Designs: www.elkhorndesigns.com
- Ethan Allen: www.ethanallen.com
  (a must-visit site, excellent values)
- Expressions: www.expressions-furniture.com
  (wonderful concept stores)
- Franklin Furniture: www.franklincf.com
- Frederick Duckloe & Bros: www.duckloe.com
- From The Crate: www.straightfromthecrate.com
- Furniture Care: www.furniturecare.com
- Furniture City: www.furniturecity.com
- Furniture Works: www.furnitureworks.com
- Garden Cottage: www.gardencottage.com
- Gems-Beads: www.gems-beads.com
- George Smith: www.georgesmith.com
- Golden Gate Bridge: www.ggbridge.com
- Green Goddess: www.greengoddess.com
- H. Wilson Company: www.hwilson.com
- Hill Country Experience: www.hillcountryexp.com
- Home 123: www.home123furniture.com
- Home Furnishings: www.homefurnishings.com
- Images Furniture: www.imagesfurniture.com
- Jim Boles Design: www.boles-design.com
- Kauffman Wood: www.kauffmanwood.com
- Ken's Kustom Designs: www.kenskustom.com
- Kinion Furniture: www.kinionfurniture.com
- Klimesh Ornamental: www.klimesh.com
- Limn: www.limn.com
- Living Country: www.livingcountry.com
- Lodge Craft: www.lodgecraft.com
- Loft Beds: www.loftbeds.com

Furniture Web Sites with a Catalog Program and Most Often a Store Program but No Sales On Line (cont.)

- Made Rite Rocker: www.madrite.com
- Majestic Wood Works: www.majwood.com
- Merridian: www.merridian.com
- Murphy's Gallery: www.murph.com
- New England Boat: www.boatfurniture.com (for the specialists)
- New West Furniture: www.newwest.com
- Nino Madia: www.ninomadiafurniture.com
- Oriental Depot: www.orientaldepot.com
- Originals in Wood: www.originalsinwood.com
- Osborne Wood: www.osbornewood.com
- PC Innovations: www.pcinnov.com
- Rose Furniture: www.rosefurniture.com (one of North Carolina's Big Four, a favorite of mine)
- Rustique: www.rustique.com
- Safriet's Furniture: www.safrietfurniture.com
- Sedital: www.sedital.com
- Shaker Shops West: www.shakershops.com (Shaker/country is always interesting)
- Signature Interiors: www.signatureinteriors.com
- Simply Together: www.simplytogether.com
- Southwestern: www.southwesternfurniture.com
- Teak Antiquity: www.teak-antiquity.com
- Telescope Casual: www.telescopecasual.com
- Tidewater: www.tidewaterworkshop.com
- Totem: www.totemdesign.com
- UnPainted Place: www.unpaintedplace.com
- Virtual Seating: www.virtualseating.com
- Wood Carver: www.woodcarverinc.com
- Wood Technology: www.wood-tech.com

chapter 6

Specialty Furniture

The Internet is also a wonderful place to find information on specialty furniture. Two such categories are office furniture and antiques. Acquiring pieces of these types of furniture can be labor-intensive, as you plod from office retailer to office retailer (or antiques shop to tag sale) to find something that suits your fancy.

Office Furniture

Not only are the computer and Internet opening up a new world in shopping, they are redefining even where we will be doing our work. Home offices, even now an important part of many homes, will become even more critical in the near term as the hub of a family's computer activities. We will be needing more and more office furniture, but currently most traditional furniture stores feature very little office furniture on their floors. Big office retailers like Office Max show significant amounts of merchandise for sale, but most of it is standard size, standard quality, standard standard. Bless its heart, even the Internal Revenue Service is changing its position on the home office, which should allow many of us to get a tax break on where we work at home. Always remember to check current rules with your accountant. To open up the options, I am listing a number of Internet office furniture sources here.

Web Sites Featuring Office Furnishings

- A-1 Office Furnishings: www.a1office.com
- ABCO Office Furniture: www.abcofurniture.com
- Alan Desk: www.alandesk.com
- Ally Office Furniture: www.allyfurn.com
- Amotek: www.amotek.com
- Ares Line: www.aresline.com
- Astron Comdesk: www.comdesk.com
- B & I Furniture: www.bi-furniture.com
- B&H Furniture Systems: www.bhfurniture.com
- Berk's Office Furniture: www.berks.com
- BioFit Seating: www.bioengseat.com
- Brayton International: www.4brayton.com
- Brook Furniture Rental: www.bfr.com
- Bush Furniture: www.bushdirect.com
- Capital Interiors: www.capitaloffice.com
- ORT Rental: www.cort1.com
- Creative Seatings: www.have-a-seat.com
- Creative Supports: www.creativesupports.com
- Crest Office Furniture: www.crestoffice.com
- Custom Installations: www.custominstall.com
- Cyber Chair: www.cyberchair.com
- Dauphin Seating: www.dauphin.com
- Delta Furniture: www.deltafurniture.com
- Designs, Furniture & Install: www.dfiinc.com
- Eagle Chair: www.eaglechair.com
- Eakes Office Plus: www.eakes.com
- Encore Systems: www.encoreusa.com
- Enviro Furniture: www.esfi.com
- Environmental Interiors: www.envint.com
- Epic Design Studios: www.epicdesign.com
- Facilities Group: www.facgrp.com
- Fashion Furniture: www.fashionfurniture.com
- Felco Office Systems Co: www.felco.com
- Fuller Furniture: www.fulleroffice.com

Web Sites Featuring Office Furnishings   (cont.)

- Furniture Express: www.f-ex.com
- Furniture Forum: www.furniture-office.com
- GF Furniture: www.gfoffice.com
- Hamilton Sorter: www.hamiltonsorter.com
- Haworth Furniture: www.haworth-furn.com
- Herman Miller: www.hermanmiller.com
- Home Office Furniture: www.hofs.com
- John Thomas Assoc: www.jtassociates.com
- Jones-Campbell Co: www.jonescampbell.com
- KI: www.ki-inc.com
- Landscape Forms: www.landscapeforms.com
- La-Z-Boy: www.lzbcontract.com
- Library Bureau: www.librarybureau.com
- Lizell Furniture: www.lizell.com
- Maryland Office: www.mdofficefurn.com
- Matrix Trading Company: www.mrxt.com
- Mead-Hatcher: www.meadhatcher.com
- Meridian: www.meridian-inc.com
- Miller SQA: www.millersqa.com
- Mobilier Informatique: www.mobilo.com
- Montage: www.montageweb.com
- National Furniture: www.nflinc.com
- Office Furn. Forum: www.furniture-office.com
- Office Furniture: www.officefurniture-usa.com
- Office Liquidators: www.officeliquidators.com
- Office Products & Interiors: www.opiinc.com

Web Sites Featuring Office Furnishings   (cont.)

- Office Source: www.furnituresource.com
- Office Station: www.officestation.com
- Office USA: www.officefurniture-usa.com
- Office World: www.officeworld.com
- O'Sullivan Industries: www.furnituredirect.com
- Provintial Partitions: www.pro-part.com
- R.C. Dawson Co: www.rcdawson.com
- Repo Depo: www.repodepo.com
- Resource Alliance: www.business-furniture.com
- Rieke Office Interiors: www.rieke.com
- Sam Clar Office Furniture: www.samclar.com
- Santos Group: www.santosgroup.com
- Sligh Furniture: www.sligh.com
- Southern Enterprises: www.seidal.com
- Spacesaver Group: www.spacesaver.com
- Steelcase: www.steelcase.com
- Steeltech Electropainting: www.steeltech.com
- Tayco Panelink: www.tayco.com
- Techline: www.techline-furn.com
- The`Office: www.the-office.com
- Thornwood Furniture: www.tfmi.com
- Watson Furniture: www.cablekeeper.com
- Wieland Furniture: www.rmwieland.com
- Winsted Corp: www.winsted.com
- Woodtronics company: www.woodtronics.com

> Any time you are considering antique furniture, either "official" or simply "old" or "new/old," you really have to know what you are doing. Never buy an antique for investment purposes unless you are an expert.

Antiques on the Web

There is a great deal of interest today in antiques. The popularity of "The Antique Road Show" and related shows point to this, but, unfortunately, they may be fueling a "get rich quick" mentality that indicates fortunes can be made with antique furniture. They can be! But not by amateurs! Oh, a few will get lucky and stumble upon something that turns out to be valuable, but it is very important to keep this caution in mind: Don't buy antique furniture for profit unless you are an expert. Don't rely on antique furniture dealers to advise you on what to buy unless you are an expert. Enjoy the shops and the web sites and buy what you would like to live with if it fits your budget. Beyond that, either become an expert, or just become a lover of wonderful antique furniture for its own sake.

These are the "top 10" antique web sites as listed by www.toptenlinks.com, the web site of *Web Bound Magazine*. Both are marvelous resources to keep on hand when surfing the net in all categories. It is important to build a library of resources, both computer-based and as hard copy, so you can quickly find what you are looking for and not be a slave to overworked search engines. The Internet will work best for you when you eliminate as much random searching as you can. Add useful sites to your "favorites" file or bookmark them so they will be only a click away.

Web Sites Featuring Antiques

+ The Internet Antique Shop: www.tias.com
+ Atlantique City: www.atlantiquecity.com
+ Antiques Et Art Australia: www.antique-art.com.au
  (you are going to Australia here)
+ Ruby Lane: www.rubylane.com
+ www.antique-shop.com: www.antique-shop.com
+ Antiques Bulletin Online: www.antiquesbulletin.com
+ NADA: www.nadaweb.org
+ Portobello: www.portobelloroad.co.uk
  (you are going to Great Britain here)
+ Antique Networking: www.antiqnet.com
+ Cyber Antique Mall: www.cyberantiquemall.com

chapter 7

Paying for Furniture

I could go into detail about using cash or checks over credit cards, but the bottom line when buying over the Internet is this: Always use a credit card. If you are a cash customer, still use your credit card, and when the furniture is safely in your home and you are satisfied, pay off your credit card balance with cash. You need the credit-card transaction to give you protection and leverage when you are dealing with any merchant involving a process as potentially complicated as buying furniture. It's that simple. In fact, whether you are buying on the Internet or buying at your local store, your credit card gives you a wonderful circle of security and protection against any and all of the potential pitfalls in any transaction.

What About State and Local Taxes When Internet-Shopping?

The quick answer is that, in most cases, you do not pay any local or state sales taxes when you purchase products on the Internet. In many states you have a legal obligation to report the purchase to the proper agency, but this is between you and your conscience. This can be a substantial savings when you are considering buying several furniture items. Needless to say, state and local governments are fighting tooth and nail to change the laws in this regard, but at the moment you will not pay any sales taxes if your Internet merchant does not have a physical presence in your state. If the merchant does have a physical presence in your state, you will be obligated to pay the sales tax. All of this is not as complicated as it sounds. Anytime you are buying anything on the Internet you will be informed if the transaction is taxable. You will know, up front, if you must pay. If you are obligated for the tax, you can then judge whether the Internet purchase is a better overall value than the same or a similar product bought from a local merchant.

Are Internet Furniture Retailers the New "Out Of State" Discounters?

So much has changed and is changing in the world of furniture shopping that many old myths are being replaced by new ones. The prevailing myth is that huge savings on brand-name furniture can be had by buying from the North Carolina furniture outlets. There was a time not too long ago when this was true. Of course, the savings were often not as great as imagined once all the extras were added in, but it was true that the consumer always saved the sales tax, generally received a larger discount off the manufacturer's suggested resale price list, and came away feeling that he or she had beaten the system. However, with local retailers tightening their belts and offering larger discounts, the difference between the prices offered by North Carolina and the local stores is being reduced. Coupled with this, some major manufacturers have instituted policies restricting maximum discounts to 40 percent off the manufacturer's suggested retail price. (The number of these manufacturers is quite small, leaving about 10,000 other suppliers who simply want to sell furniture and have no restrictions on discounting.) Still, in most cases, Internet furniture retailers and the North Carolina furniture outlets still have an advantage when it comes to state and local sales taxes.

What all this means is that the Internet furniture retailer and the North Carolina furniture outlet share a similar approach to the marketplace. Both have business structures that give them a competitive advantage over many local retailers. Interestingly, they both need the local retailer as a standard and source to compete against. It isn't fair but it is business.

The new myth is that the Internet furniture retailer is going to save you tons of money. This just isn't true. To begin with, you can only save "tons of money" if you know what you are doing and can compare product to product and not brand name to brand name. It is always true that nationally advertised brand-name products will cost more than similar but more obscure products. The trick is to know a value when you see it no matter what manufacturer's name is touted. Since many major manufacturers with national distribution systems are hesitant to disrupt their relationships with local merchants, there is and will increasingly be a trend to private-label their products for sale by Internet retailers. This could prove to be a real plus for the consumer. If National Retailer X decides to sell an Internet furniture retailer a collection of furniture that is displayed in local stores under a private label, you could very well be getting the exact name-brand merchandise for significantly less money.

This will be particularly true if the Internet retailer takes less of a markup than the local merchant. And why shouldn't this happen? The Internet retailer has significantly lower overhead than a typical merchant. To begin with, the Internet retailer doesn't have that brick-and-mortar store to pay for. There are no salespeople to finance. The Internet retailer may well have no inventory and few or no display costs. The list goes on and on and the savings could be a real boon to consumers.

But there is a catch. Will you recognize the private label merchandise for what it really is? Probably not. However, if you do your homework, you will probably recognize the added details on a piece of furniture that add value for the price and buy accordingly. You will not need to know brand names if you know your stuff.

My first book, *Shopping For Furniture: A Consumer's Guide*, published by Linden Publishing Company in 1999, goes into considerable detail on what to look for when buying upholstered or wood furniture. I have given a great deal of detail in this book on what to look for and what to ask for when you are shopping the Internet retailer. It will be harder for you to consider the details when you are shopping the Internet, since you will not be seeing the furniture in the flesh so to speak. This is the downside of Internet shopping. On this point alone, North Carolina furniture outlets and local stores offer a distinct advantage. At the very least, the outlets can provide a price benchmark—you will know what the bottom price is for the vast majority of furniture that is available in the marketplace, and this knowledge will be a powerful shopping tool. The promised great savings that the Internet myth speaks to will continue to be a myth unless conditions change and shoppers become smart.

Web Site Addresses for North Carolina Furniture Outlets

- Alman's Home Furnishings: www.almanfurniture.com
- American Reproductions: www.americanreproductions.com
- The Atrium: www.theatrium.com
- Beacon Hill Factory Outlet: www.hickoryfurniture.com
- Better Homes Discount Furniture: www.bhdf.com
- Blackwelders: www.homefurnish.com/blackwelders
- Blowing Rock Furniture Co: www.blowingrockfurniture.com
- Bonita Furniture Galleries: www.hfnet.com/bonita.html
- Boyles Country Shop: www.boyles.com
- Braddington Young Gallery: www.blowingrockfurniture.com
- Broyhill Showcase Gallery: www.hickoryfurniture.com
- Carolina Furniture of Williamsburg: www.carolina-furniture.com
- Carolina Patio Warehouse: www.carolinapatio.com
- Cayton Furniture: www.caytonfurniture.com
- Century Factory Outlet: www.hickoryfurniture.com
- Collector's Furniture Gallery: www.acollectorsgallery.com
- Council-Craftsman Factory Outlet: www.hickoryfurniture.com
- Don Lamor: www.donlamor.com
- Drexel-Heritage Factory Outlet: www.hickoryfurniture.com
- Drexel-Heritage Factory Outlet: www.furniturelandsouth.com
- Ellenburg's Furniture: www.ellenburgs.com
- French Heritage Factory Store: www.theatrium.com
- Furniture Collections of Carolina: www.users.twave.net/fcc/
- The Furniture Shoppe: www.furnitureshoppe.com
- FurnitureLand South: www.furniturelandsouth.com
- Gordon's Furniture Store: www.ncnet.com/ncnw/gordons.html
- Green Front Furniture: www.greenfront.com
- Henredon Factory Outlet: www.hickoryfurniture.com
- Hickory Chair Factory Outlet: www.hickoryfurniture.com
- Hickory Park Furniture Galleries: www.hickorypark.com

Web Site Addresses for North Carolina Furniture Outlets (cont.)

- Home Focus: www.homefocusfurniture.com
- Homeway Furniture: www.homewayfurniture.com
- Hudson Discount Furniture: www.hudsonfurniture.com
- Ironstone Galleries Factory Outlet: www.hickoryfurniture.com
- Kagan's American Drew: www.www.theatrium.com
- Kincaid Galleries: www.kincaidgalleries.com
- La Barge Factory Outlet: www.hickoryfurniture.com
- Lindy's Furniture Co: www.lindysfurniture.com
- Loftin Black Furniture Co: www.ncnet.com/ncnw/tho-loft.html
- Maitland-Smith Factory Outlet: www.hickoryfurniture.com
- Mallory's Fine Furniture: www.mallorys.com
- Monroe's Furniture: www.monroesfurniture.com
- Morgan Stewart Galleries: www.msgalleries.com
- Nite Furniture Co: www.ncnet.com/ncnw/nite.html
- Pennsylvania House Gallery: www.theatrium.com
- Quality Furniture Market of Lenoir: www.qualityfurnituremarket.com
- Repete's: www.hfnet.com/repetes/
- Rhoney Furniture Clearance Center: www.hickoryonline.com/rhoneyfurniture
- Robert Bergelin Co: www.rbcfurn.com
- Rooms Now: www.furniturelandsouth.com
- Rose Furniture: www.rosefurniture.com
- Rose Furniture Main Clearance Center: www.roseclearance.com
- Shaw Furniture Galleries: www.shawfurniture.com
- Southern Designs: www.hickoryfurniture.com
- Stevens Furniture: www.stevensfurniture.com
- Thomas Home Furnishings: www.hfnet.com/thf.html
- Thomasville Factory Outlet: www.thomasville.com
- Wellington's Fine Leather Furniture: www.fineleatherfurniture.com
- Wood Armfield Furniture Co: www.theatrium.com
- Zagaroli Classics: www.zagarolileather.com

Chapter 7 Paying for Furniture

NOTE: You probably have noticed that many of the web sites list the name "hickoryfurniture" in the web address. This indicates that they have showroom space at The Hickory Furniture Mart in Hickory, North Carolina. The Mart's phone number is 1-800-462-MART if you are having trouble running around on the web sites. The Mart is a huge building complex, representative of the trend to bundle large groups of outlets under one roof to make shopping easier. The North Carolina discount outlet scene has come a long way from the days of small, independent, widely separated retailers doing business in a building piled high with crates and a single phone. Retailers no longer load their warehouses to the rafters with stock furniture. No one in the business can afford to carry heavy inventories, nor can manufacturers afford to make many production mistakes. The computer, again, is coming to the rescue. Planning is better than ever and mistakes are fewer, but no system is perfect and there will always be a need for manufacturers to get rid of their furniture problems. This is a legitimate need and is recognized by all segments of the furniture industry.

Problem furniture is made up of a number of factors: flat-out manufacturing mistakes, returned merchandise from customers, soiled or damaged products, discontinued merchandise, etc. These pieces carry the big, seductive discounts. In day-to-day discounts on regular running merchandise, you can expect discounts ranging from 30 to 50 percent, although the majority of items will probably carry a discount of 40 percent off the manufacturer's suggested retail price. All these outlets, for the most part, are showing regular, problem-free merchandise on their floors. The smart shopper will contact, investigate, and consider buying merchandise from a North Carolina furniture outlet. I never thought I would say that. What has changed?

The Internet plus the North Carolina furniture outlet offers a powerful combination of strengths that has never existed before. Let's face it. Before the Internet, the North Carolina connection was an occasional intrusion into the life of the average furniture retailer. The North Carolina connection was and is more than an occasional problem for any retail dealer East of Denver, but it rarely posed a problem for Western dealers. But with the Internet and the North Carolina furniture outlet web sites, consumers have the opportunity to explore more choices at better prices. The combination is unbeatable.

What about the dealers who have invested thousands of dollars to bring furniture to you in your town? Don't they deserve some consideration and support? In a sense, yes. The people running these dealerships are your neighbors, but remember that any business must be competitive or face the consequences. Too many furniture insiders forget that they must make consumers happy, not dealers. This simple point is often forgotten in the hand-wringing that goes on when furniture insiders talk about change.

Is the Internet Retailer Going To "Kill" Your Local Retailer?

A lot of local retailers think so. History tells us time and again that people who cannot or will not adapt to change and turn it to their advantage are left behind by new ideas, new techniques, new demands. In a collective sense, the consumer rules. Even though you may think you don't matter in the great sweep of change, as part of a collective whole you matter very much, for the collective decision of any group picks the winners and losers in any category. Without question, Internet retailers and retailing will profoundly change traditional brick-and-mortar retailers. Competition from Internet retailers will make local merchants better, more consumer-focused, with better service, better prices, better help from sales personnel, and better displays. Furniture stores will introduce excitement and theater into the equation so that shopping will be more interesting and informative. The local merchant who doesn't take his or her business apart and restructure it into a more exciting retailing adventure for the consumer will be doomed—and rightly so.

No business is entitled to profits and survival if that business is not determined to give customers the best values and the best experience possible. It is that simple. I'm not talking about selling merchandise at such low prices that the dealer has to go out of business. Look at all the examples of businesses that charge more than the next guy and people are still beating down the doors to get in. Why? They are succeeding in spite of being higher priced because they are offering not just a product but an event, an experience, a dream, something extra that people will pay more for.

Chapter 7 Paying for Furniture

Every day in the furniture-trade publications you hear cries of protest from traditional retailers that Internet retailers are not playing fair. They don't have to collect sales taxes, they don't have high overhead, they don't need to keep big inventories for delivery, they don't need to pay large sales forces, and so on. Of course it isn't fair. But the whole purpose of business is to find a competitive advantage that allows you to undercut your competition and still make a profit while giving the consumer everything he or she wants. This is what free enterprise is all about. Now in all fairness, it is necessary to consider the argument that businesses provide the tax base that sustains much of what our society collectively needs to run government and all it entails. It is a solid point. We need all businesses to carry their fair share of the burden of providing all the goods and services we need, but this argument is generally a smoke screen that ignores the more basic question of how each individual business conducts itself relative to its customers. I see a new kind of local store—a local store connected to the Internet in new and exciting ways; a local store with an Internet workstation that will multiply limited floor space by the almost infinite scope of the Internet. Consumers will not exist in a cyber-vacuum, cut off from the real joy of experiencing home furnishings as they exist in all the glory of a perfect blend of function and art, of utility and magic. I also see more informed designers and salespeople who, with the assistance of the Internet, will be able to find immediate answers to questions. I see sales personnel who can tap into the design expertise of major data banks and still provide the human touch that can make any experience better. I see an industry evolving—and I see the Internet bringing all the elements together for the ultimate benefit of the consumer. Finally there is a vehicle that can show the scope and richness of the furniture industry, unhampered by competitive manufacturers, who had to fight over expensive and limited floor space. Finally there is developing a marketplace that can hold all of the home furnishings industry in its hand, and is accessible to all consumers at the click of a mouse.

> In 1994 (which is a lifetime ago in Internet time), David Cole, the chairman of KSA Management Consulting in Atlanta, predicted that consumers would enter stores already equipped with exhaustive details about product and prices. He went on to say that he expected that "by 2010, non-store retailing will account for more than half of consumer sales."

A Final Word

The Internet and all that it entails is the most revolutionary, most exciting tool to come our way since the telephone. Like the telephone, the Internet in itself contributes nothing to our lives until we pick it up and use it. The potential of great benefit is there, but potential benefits rarely affect us in any way until the tool is used. Within five years I would expect most of the furniture-buying Western world to be online. In a very short time, we will be connected to every corner of the world.

Leonard B. Lewin

Fair Oaks, CA

Spring 2000

Contact numbers for Leonard B. Lewin

4917 St Thomas Drive

Fair Oaks, CA 95628

916-966-0215 (office)

916-966-7838 (fax)

lewin@foothill.net (personal email)

www.furnitureideas.com (web site)

Notes

Notes

Notes

Notes